SIGHT

Lyn Hejinian
&
Leslie Scalapino

EDGE

Cover design by Ree Hall
Typesetting by Barbara Campbell

Sections of this work, in somewhat different versions, have appeared in *Sojourner, parataxis, Black Bread, Prosodia, Shambala Sun, Global City, Raddle Moon, Lingo, Proliferation, Zyzzyva, Private Arts, A Salt Reader, No Roses, River City,* and *The Bellingham Review,* the authors sincerely thank the editors of these journals.

Two segments from Leslie Scalapino's part were published first in *The Front Matter, Dead Souls* (Wesleyan University Press, 1996).

We also wish to express our appreciation to Robert Grenier for his exemplary work with text as sight.

ISBN: 1-890311-06-5

Edge Books
P.O. Box 25642
Washington, DC 20007

Edge Books are published by *Aerial* magazine.

Sight

Experience / 'On' Sight

We agreed that the form of our collaboration was to be in doubles, pairs (such as two sentences, two lines or paragraphs, or series of these, etc.); and that the subject, being sight, should involve things actually seen. Multiple pairs and crossing the borders of these occur: which are friendship / thought / sight itself / events …

Crossing 'across' observation, 'argument' which is mode of extension — we tend to stay on our own 'sides' in regard to the 'subject' 'experience.' We attempt to draw each other across the sides of our 'argument' or boundary, a form of pairs, and of friendship also. We sign our segments, which are sometimes like letters as specifically referring to occasion and to writing. 'Critical discourse' as they say, in which the poetry is interchangeable as the thought in it. Sometimes, seeing in real events we had to turn seeing up to an extreme in order to see it; as if dreaming being suppressed were bursting out as luminous seeing in the waking state. Pairs of sights, become that by being placed beside each other; my dreaming speaking to you (a pairing of you), I put in as part of the collaboration.

Friendship would have to be not just 'being liked.' That one has to be likable, accommodating. One would have to 'like' also — i.e. like the other — and I think only *by* being oneself. Not accommodating. My need for argument in it is that you tend to view reality as wholesome; when I'm suffering you tend to alleviate to bring suffering into the currency of the 'social,' the realm that is convivial — whereas I'm saying it's (also) apprehension itself when it's occurring.

The accumulation of pairings as 'extreme' sights occurs to the extent of being as if the writing's faculty, rather than being imaginative images.

I dreamt while we were collaborating that I spat in a donkey's eye (in the future, but already known) and rushed up (before this) to tell you that 'all of life was void,' which I knew in the dream you would want to hear. Because I was indicating that to spit in the donkey's eye (not to have to be accommodating) was the gesture, being done; that gesture also being the act of friendship and apprehension.

So, anyway — I tend to say that experience is scrutiny; that it is 'travel' in the sense of dislocation of one's own perspective (that is, not to have a perspective). You say to me then: "travel is sentimental." In other words, I'm deluding myself that I could ever not have a perspective. It is my 'doctrine' only. (You're right. I agree, it was not scrutiny enough.) When I 'discuss' "compassion," you check me. That such (in that form at least) is egotism or a 'lyrical illusion,' probably.

Then, on my part, I thought recently you described (at the university) your writing in terms of ideas — that it is "comparing cultures" — which will be accepted as description of the writing (its importance) but which is not the gesture that occurs *as* the writing (the mind coming up with whatever it is at that moment only). (Acknowledgment that it's perspective only.) Because you know the professors will tend not to like the 'idea' of the mind as only its action at a moment, because they don't trust that. It isn't 'any thing.' 'Writing separate from and being then people's activity' is one of the subjects of Sight.

As doubles or pairings: The description as what people will like is not the way the thing (the event or writing) *is*.

The writing that's occurring at any point is the entire body of writing. Of others, as well. So the writing of a time is everyone.

A 'time' is the work being written at the time by everyone. It is not the hierarchy of what people regard. In that accumulation transforms.

I want friendship that's real, because it occurs only. (This was Lear's mistake — or maybe it was Cordelia's — ? — they seem to be part of the same person. I was re-writing *King Lear* in a recent work of mine, called *As: All Occurrence in Structure, Unseen — (Deer Night)*, which I was doing alongside *Sight*. I was also writing *The Front Matter, Dead Souls*. Passages of mine originating in *Sight* got into *The Front Matter* as being alongside it. In the latter, I was working on visual extremity as the writing literally as if a faculty, rather than visual being imagination.)

In such an approach — (if there's a division between description and text — you're pointing away from there being a text, from reading) you're not comparing cultures because you're indicating in a sense 'the real' is 'the social,' what is liked — else it is lyrical illusion.

Yet, to be "comparing cultures" — cannot occur from a standpoint that is an insulated one in which reality is described as (one's) halcyon/ "normal" (by such description regarded as objective in regard to culture and thought, as what is seen to be "intellectual" *per se*). Comparing cultures cannot occur as that, reality or cultures not being subject to 'halcyon'/ 'normal.' Apprehension as comparison isn't there then, because it's generalized. Were it there, that would be dis-locating. It (apprehension /conflict — the same?) isn't there. The point is not that one is suffering because of being dislocated — but that the thought *is* the action.

So you're (one's) 'being removed from experience' as that *being* (if that's one's) definition of objectivity or apprehension itself — whereas apprehension only *exists* as experience?

Leslie Scalapino

We embarked on this collaboration with a very general project in mind, and one that seemed to develop many facets and suggest many possible developments as we proceeded with it. In the broadest sense, we were interested in a joint investigation into the working of experience: how experience happens, what it consists of, how the experiencing (perceiving, feeling, thinking) of it occurs, what the sensation of sensing tells us. And we were interested in knowing what actual experiences would take place over the period of time we would be working on the collaboration — what would happen in our respective lives and what would happen between us, in public (as the writing) and in private (as a flourishing friendship).

Another way to characterize the project would be to describe it as a work of acknowledgement. This is a theme which is also a prominent one in *A Border Comedy,* the work that I was writing concurrently with *Sight,* and elements from *A Border Comedy* appear in this book, most obviously in the passages which mention a "border guard' (a figure which you, at some point, change to a "boundary guard," producing a clearer trope, and one that is more 'self'-reflexive).

In *Sight* we attempt to acknowledge the world simply by seeing it but also by stating that something has been seen. To do this, we carry on an activity (a continuous action); we are in motion, turning *toward* (things between us). Hence the inward motion. There isn't very much here that could be described as exposition — not much turning out or putting out.

From the outset, we agreed that for the purposes of this collaboration (and at some early point, do you remember just when?, we agreed that we should do other collaborations when this was completed), the question of experiencing the world would focus on sight — on the question of 'seeing': seeing the world, seeing something in it, and being in it as one whose particpation involved such "seeing." The thrill of acknowledgment (it is, after all, good to be alive!), while being addressed to what we saw, was also, over and over again, in real time, addressed to each other. Thanks to your suggestion that we 'sign' (with our initials) our passages (poems) to each other, this is a dialogic work — a joint research undertaken through conversation, and as such it includes demands, either express or internalized, for clarification, it includes debate, and it reveals changes of view under each other's influence.

Our only constraint was that each response — each poem — would have two parts and that in each poem there should be some reference to, or presentation of, something actually seen. But we never limited the scope of what might be considered a sight or sighting. And I, at least, included occasional dream images and many other purely mental pictures, concentrating in particular on those mental pictures (sometimes logical, sometimes seemingly inappropriate) that seemed to flash into view in response to your words. This wasn't a form of mind-reading — that would have been invasive and I think we share a dislike of such mental power games. It was phenomenological — our ideas took shape for each other, though in ways that were probably idiosyncratic to each of us.

As I look at this work now in retrospect, I see it as elaborating problems in phenomenology but not in description, and this, given our topic, seems curious. Of course description is often phenomenological in intent — aimed at bringing something into view, trying to replicate for (or produce in) the reader an experience of something seen. But it seems as if our emphasis was not on the thing seen but on the coming to see. As I see it, this book argues that the moment of coming to see is active and dialogic, and as such it is dramatic.

Many things were seen during the course of our writing this book. And now I hope that some reader will see something in it — not through it but in it. Sight is not transparent. But the best conditions for seeing are not always clear.

Lyn Hejinian

Sight

This conscious attempt to see is producing sensations of searching
　　As in a museum — or walking off balance, hurrying forward in order to compensate for the weight of my eyes and even then leaning — I am drawn from one thing to another

(LH)

　　　　pool of lagoon moving
　　　　　　doesn't occur

　　its rim's in the newspaper even.
　　　　　　it's completely clear with a mountain in it. and not
　　　　　　generating memory. it's *just* memory actually. won't
　　　　　　accept his bullying however promulgated by them
　　　　　　ever

(LS)

　　But I accept a greeting at a place I've never seen, leaning toward the wind, as someone moving forward is coming to mind — and the moment itself is being remembered at the same instant, with the event recognized
　　At a beach with breakers, in the absence of whatever there is between anything and me

(LH)

Thin silver disc moon shredded at the bottom edge is
　　　　seen in late day. it has a fringe that's shredded and seen a few days ago. But not memory as a function to see.

One's seeing it today when it has occurred really before, and not using memory for it.
　　　　Memory occurs on its own.
　　　　One's seeing it anyway, as if in or by forgetting,
　　　　rather than at the time of its occurring
　　　　It occurs then but is seen

now on blue evening which doesn't exist.
I only remember it later, but am seeing it by forgetting
       later and while it's occurring
       Silver moon disc in blue occurs in the separation

                                                                             (LS)

       And then this seeing is not a silent proceeding
       I've hung a man in the upper branches of the tree and he's
expected to sing to me
       But in the interval between that sight and this expectation
(the spectre prolongs this interval) I change my memory, and the
sight to which I've referred (in memory) recurs as another sight

       The faster we go, the nearer we are to the trees

                                                                             (LH)

The shredding at the lower rim of disc of
       moon is in the separation
       by its not being remembered when it's happening

       I have to remember its event of coming to the trees of
       occurring then but is seen now
              to have fights inside
(of others)
              (this is a shape, a clamor or sometimes silent shape,
not a sight. Occurs interiorly while seeing, beginning before that
other seen object or place)
             where that exists

                                                                   (LS)

       The moon (or moon event) is evaporating through
binoculars, penetrable, billowing behind the wind, and leaves
curling, under the tree hurled and released back against the wall,
material under the tree and more audible if I look carefully through
the dark, but whipped past it over and over again, within something

---

4

it borders
     The shredding at that border's edge is a kind of trail or
prophecy — something we *might* see — and lose, because everything exists

                                                               (LH)

Seeing occurs from using on it what doesn't have that capacity in it
                as solely public
     Blindly white gazing, so that the recipient of it isn't
existing inside — and is still fighting. Not seeing is flagellating inside
— actual real moon sliver as memory only when it's being seen
           One can't not dream
                 which isn't seeing. There isn't *other* in it
                    dreaming not having memory either

                                                              (LS)

           The desire to see, and *thus* to be oblivious (not a self),
guiltlessly, a simple eye, makes the blank on which we *can* see
     The moon's in public
     It's for verification
     Has repetitions, keeping, in divided (shared) memory

     Thrashing
     To see that it's stable, self-similar, still
     Is its presence then innocuous? put aside because we're
similar? being seen?
     But I desire to see being remembered as having seen

                                                               (LH)

To be observant and not seeing oneself
        and be remembered seeing
by oneself
        is eliminated continually as a blazing assembly
        who're alive though some are asleep
        and see brightly there
        I wake up and they're there.

Clouds, independently
They blaze — they keep to an assemblage which is not an
illusion

The clouds of anything I've seen today I remember in a
clasping gaze
It's an inadequate perception though I might see that thing
again (and that is essential to the objective beauty of its clouds)
The sleep of my experience wakes in the stream of
anything's existence — I am leaning there

(LH)

that being alive is the same
as if one were after dying
the moon returns
                in that seeing is only memory
                but not having memory when seeing it
                inducing our manipulated perception
                as the conditions and grounds for the moon's
                occurring there.

manipulated is solely public
                one's limbs float out dragging in it

(LS)

Out of the loose dirt glossy ants swarm suddenly over a
solitary centipede, writhing, coiling, but it drags them — my
watching is vicious and close but objective, then my interference is
subjective (removing the centipede)
                What's not worth manipulation becomes quotidian, private
                All previous faces, by default — lived past
                We're in a lost public

There an unfamiliar old man stops with a hand glass and
holds it over the interior parts of a flower

(LH)

Going out, homeless men are sitting
from far away here and there at their posts
young students are walking in spring
        My seeing them as if they are reflections
        of my inner self to see that
        is a minute approach
        to whom — clear

— you for example
Chaucer knew spring
if we're in a lost public
agonizing objectively is stilled

(LS)

        The television drags it home but there's not much left of it
        Blue but flesh, swarms — these are divided — by the
hesitation to stare
        The mailman removing his hat to peer through the slot in
the door seeming obsequious but with no anecdote attached — just
an enormous clean white dog
        As anyone can see — the muddled flower was an implosion
        And the memory of it is a microcosm with its own periphery
        People having gone out to have a sight (and an ant crawls
out of it)

        A thousand yellow birds flew out of my eyes when I looked
at the trees

(LH)

        People having gone out to have a sight — it can't be
hindered by that — a huge white dog appearing — the sight is the

reverse of the occurrence

If translated it's converted back to their seeing from its new
syntax — a thousand yellow birds' seeing: as people's 'not having' an
anecdote — sight is its reverse.

(LS)

     One thing seen blindly is meeting another — a white airplane
and two diapered toddlers — they are staring up at it while off-
balance under the pilot's oblivion
     He is beyond critique
     These visions are staggered
     The children go through a hoop to see what's beyond it to
parody development
     Which is a superb imitation (reflection) of what's in it

     One might simply say: arouse doubts in me
               you know that that's the sky
               an airplane cannot cease to be conceivable
               I've seen a ghost which agreed with reality

(LH)

     The crowd is on the stream — the moon's bulb flowing —
where alongside it the hyenas running pull some from out of the
stream.

     The brightened crowd lit walks beside the pack tearing and
shredding.
     They have nothing inside to move them or coming to them
to produce it. They are right where that is. Nothing to sustain it
floats: as, no imitation.
     The hyenas are on the other side of the stream, by the
crowd. Seeing two things on the stream.

(LS)

Seeing neither thugs nor astronomers
They are carefully shadowed, in the morning a floating pink
index card with a phrase inscribed in running ink and that afternoon
a lizard
In the same cafe where the lizard is seen are news
personalities flicking white cards, seeking anonymity
We are sophisticated and it is they who are ominous — the
future is empty — a great lid slides
The eye will panic if something occurs

There may be no animal boundary — just the stream and the
pleasure that lies in it
Flowing forms outside of us
Blazing energetic span

(LH)

The people sitting out and the lizard seen are as if two, on
the stream. Arbitrarily. They're meeting yet far apart. The street is
very empty because of summer. Without anything in one, there's an
image not sustained flowing, the day in which it is is lidless.
Is it, that the crowd flowing crossing is in a stream is torn
by the hyenas that come by, as they're occurring, there.

The eye will panic if something occurs. We're children still
it's anonymity. Only. There's nothing inside lit and lit dogs pass with
people on the street reflected on them.

(LS)

On the tin
            — time
reflecting a man
            selling pencils —
the street
            floats a shadow

The jerking of savage cartoons flows
Speak, says someone whom we can picture

A young woman, a mediocre violinist, is encouraging her dog to howl like an infant and she witnesses its shifting posture, its soft short hairs vibrating

On the surface spectacle
the glare of the stream
disguises the flow of malice

A woman comes in from the fog — busily, or with a schedule, or her duties must be accomplished according to a schedule, like those of a mail carrier
She is visibly grinding her teeth
If anyone is to witness anything, he or she too must have traits
We position each other — with lizard, with fiddle, with shadows, with omens — and so forth

(LH)

A meanness coming out only at the lids so that they're lidless in the hot blazing blue — in the day — is only seen. No mind in one in order to see them lidless hanging in the blue as they come up the street, long legs on a woman stalks floats through some people. She's climbing when squeezed in the beadless lid, that are their eyes on the sacks floating up to some.

Seeing people as the gel flesh sacks out that are barely translucent as such, there is no mind in one or them. They're on the street which is exactly the same as vision motions in a dream I'm having at night, where they're not there, not about anything but the motions. No one reacts in day. The eye panics if something happens, at night dreaming?

(LS)

An entirely new forest has erupted during the night replacing the older one which contained younger trees. The thin trunks of young trees always bend sharply when half-submerged in clear water just as waking life and dream life form angles where they touch. We see things without transition. Panic comes from projected memory, expectation of what's about to be seen.

A parade, its finale out of sight, passes by, led by people in a crowd carrying fruits and followed by women in green on stilts. There are things never seen which we cause to be fearful because we are ominous. We see one thing after another in the parade — the women in middle age on stilts after the fruit and a hook-and-ladder truck after the women. An entire band on a flat bed. Relentless as surf the parade repeats on another street.

(LH)

I feel depressed spatially — which is what that is — by a parade. What you write is translated in me as seen, I feel I can't see anything. Boiling day is at evening. So birds are at evening. Evening's hot on the lawn the birds running on it. People in parade are flattened and the eye is in someone crouching squatting; one's the eye of a toad where an eye as if moving on its surface flicks slowly where the woman on stalks that are her own legs was seen climbing as if flowing on them, people in a crowd.

Sleep is on a narrow level. Sleep can be united to itself, so that the dreams in it can be seen objectively once the activity that's 'real' of the day is seen to be the same narrow level or line (as the dreams). A man dressed as a Buddhist monk (who isn't that) is taken in a flat boat from a sand spit on which are piles of corpses, unburied, really of his own soldiers, not of those rowing him away. That's what I think when I read your sentence "I dreamed of an expanse of lawn with a carefully trimmed edge along which a deadly white grain was flowing. It flowed over my face." That what I see doesn't come — originally? — from me is the same as your/some other's dream. Where I didn't dream the birds being at evening. There there's no rest. One's thought is entirely seen, by everyone. Also, *only* seen. That is like not being able to sleep, sleep is eliminated.

(LS)

This wakefulness is cold, private
The vision — weak, sleeping
    by day behind blind, negligent faculties
        — of the dazzling white sand bar
                in summer
      isolated in a deep stream
          is painful, stimulating desire
The observer is searching in this relativity
She is not painting clouds

These observations are innocent, the flow of them revealing more than the sudden sincerity with which the sunlight makes them visible, the shock of the bright glare leaving something behind, lost — never vanishing

It's not guilty knowledge that allows one to see what one didn't see — many vantage points are occupied while I dream — but knowledge is always occurring in every correspondence, in this relationship, in wakefulness

(LH)

In burning days there isn't a level but I still am believing there that my parents (or his) can't die, that I can and will (but not him) but that this burning hot day is elsewhere from them where everything's let in on a narrow tunnel or hole to this plain. Where I was walking this evening in a thick rain soaking me a thin sky with the moon swimming in a clear space occurred so there's no relation to the or a day, it's bipolar.

Wind (in the rain) blew me so I couldn't look up before the moon was hanging then there. If they can die it's not that there's this barren hot plain through which the hole leads, the moon swimming ahead, two women who are musicians with a narrow glee that's real joy playing buoyant flickering to play their composition for me I began laughing loud and they're interested hearing the sound that I can laugh gauging and real sheen from them 'blissfully' as they're sawing the violin, walking there's an opening playing on land the opening itself wallowing.

      that the observations are innocent is what floats that
      is only from them

                isolated in a deep stream
                that's day-night bipolar

                                                        (LS)

        The nearby sky is intimate, ominous, erotic — the sky is
observant and the depressed area is humid, languid
        It is filled with sad dog eyes
        The sky's watchfulness is fluid, remembering nothing
        It is only immediate — or we are the immediate ones,
numerous as cups
        Pain remembers, and being psychological is circular,
sharpening memories into events
        The gorgeous swelling bounding full moon stripped of
cloud moves
        Buzzing

        Out of the potted plant flies a nesting finch by the kitchen
door
        Therefore we avoid the kitchen door — a word like
'therefore' becomes protective, parental
        The red tongue of the garter snake in the back wall is
replicated by a flicker crossing the full moon
        My parents are pleased
        There's hardly any age difference between day and night

                                                        (LH)

        This has to do with watchful attention and care for one's
parents — I don't think we remember anything
        The gorgeous swelling bounding full moon stripped of
cloud moves off in the rest.
                When there isn't a plain through which the hole leads
one doesn't even exist.
                The land and the bounding moon wallow together
                One clings to them.
                The sky's watchfulness is fluid, remembering
nothing, therefore a bipolar separation is in nature, has no relation
to one's own mind, isn't in the mind as if it's not nature.

                            ———

                            13

Then one could rest, as if one didn't have to, aware
of faculty of resting which only is it
Not being that only one will die, when that isn't
what's groundless, they're doing so is groundless.

(LS)

The dying are included — this has to be implied by living
In the focus between (an open parkland in the background,
blurred trees) there's interference, a muting of light achieved,
ghostly heat like that drifting down the beach
Disparity and asymmetry develop as ethical categories
Justice *is* inconclusive

a startling sound — merely
the whap of a flailing kid cannonballing
— creates a completely different picture

a chord signifying an upholstered chair

someone named in the picture
walking very precisely
because of a blind spot —
lifts his legs higher than usual
stepping over the barricade of the invisible

and the picture itself passes
out of sight — there's a bank of wild myrtle
— pungent when broken — dark green
gleaming but dry, dusty, thick
so that things could be lost if thrown there
— a yellow dog bounds into it
and falls

the flashes of light on the water adding

(LH)

Eliminating to evening, it's not seen, at it though

it's active, not stilled — as to the
woman flowing on the street climbing
(to where she's doing that)

People in lines don't fall down at
evening when it occurs, the evening.
At the movie mall the sky is huge
I'm too awake to calm down, the
              evening's yellow dog
              bounds into it, the dog not seen at it.
              Watching,
              a black butterfly can't be seen in the blue
      when it's in it.
      the black butterfly flying can't be seen in blue.

                                            (LS)

      The moon flying bright behind the cloud, engulfed, seems to
blacken it
      The blue engulfed by evening
      This is implicit in the image, background to the film, in
which a blue-hued building, bullet-shaped, is seen from a viewpoint
hugging the ground
      The perspective enlarges the monolith and the monolith
belongs to prisoners identifiable because of their banded look
      Only one person sees this if it occurs in a dream (engulfed in
sleep)

              A moth almost as large as a bat
              swoops through the nearly dark
              twilight, leaving the impression of red
              although the moth, if batlike, must be
              brown or gray, the red an effect of
              the sound it makes, the sweeping.
              Memories have the same effect, but
              they flare — blue and celebratory.
              Evening in summer. Kids hiding
              behind trees, shouting, acting out
              hostility, invisibility, deceit, playing
              "Prisoner's Base" and "Capture the

Flag" (the 'flag' is my shirt).

(LH)

Dreaming that a man, loved, (who really disappeared)
reappears to live with one as if it will obliterate the relationship with
the man, loved with whom one lives,
>> though it shouldn't as he's *cared for* (the one who
disappeared)
>> 'one's' only conflict
>> one's younger brother doesn't exist. So I have the
sensation that it's better that he *has* existed.
>> We're sleeping (while I'm dreaming) worn out as if
kneeling — were going to rise at 5:30 to see the
convergence of a red giant star with Venus, but couldn't
emersed.
>> The blue greenish Venus comes close to the red star
occurring in nature when we're not seeing it.
>> Neither (it or us) is seeing or parting.

Waking to seeing
>> Huge crows on a gold plateau strutting stiffly on
their legs on the tufts of a gold plain in front of me.

Cattle are on another gold plain at evening.

Cattle are in dim fog at pools flying along the fields.
Conflict as 'one' is outside one yet isn't in the dim
cattle shreds appearing which when engulfed in blue don't
appear; they might run at dark, when it is.

(LS)

Awake at dawn, departing, a man on deck says that sailors
should never ride horses and that cowboys always drown at sea
>> Rising and falling with the lights in the pale sea
>> Gold to the fog fishing slowly
>> This is unprecedented — there are objects everywhere,
desires engulfed, at ease

Pleasure and displeasure decrease
All morning ascending the coast, reversing the concept of
"reality" by adding nothing to the "pool of information"

But the ironic disclaim nothing — the image of this unfolds,
a panorama, the full measure of degrees
    The "wise" are ecstatically watchful, regarding the big fish
    Then there's action — forming
    When really in action, the acting don't picture
    Later the image of this disappears — exhausted

(LH)

The occurrence of (you) being on a boat sailing not seeing
the sky, awake at dawn, departing, to come close to where we were
going to but didn't rise to see the red giant star draw close to Venus
didn't come from, events emerging solely
            occurring by seeing
            or effected by ordering them
            — either.

        Just touching but where the one
    doesn't produce the other.

        Not producing, occurring is seeing. It's just
appearing on its own. I see my exhaustion (having a disk injury in the
neck) at the moment: to be a purely physical 'contentless' condition,
which as such is (yet is not from) mental, as the one is of the luminous
other, the gold to the fog is your fishing slowly as an outer occurrence
is. The physical creates a state which has no mental 'place' and so no
resolution there. Arising from there not being a mental counterpart
even repressed, but that not being a state of resting. The pale sea gold
to the fog and fishing slowly is a state which has neither counterpart,
of one's mental or physical weariness, yet is a luminous outer
occurrence then apprehended and is 'apparently' only being awake at
dawn, (which I wasn't) as nothing else.
        The artificial, unnatural?, suppression of the physical state
makes the luminous event occurring in nature part.

(LS)

17

The lights on the 'weariless' foggy sea at the end of the
fishing day are sharp as knives, glinting
    Gulls in the wake churning after the viscera of the gutted
fish, always the same
    Seen the same, nothing to change — unless speaking of it
    From before dawn in the dark, figures of (mostly) drifting
men in the fog on the dock
    They are expectant, unlike ghosts, and resting
    They are sleepy but macho, ebullient in their impermeable
clumsy boots
    Boys drinking beer
    The macho is enacted nonetheless in jacketed sobriety,
booted competence, deftly threading the anchovies and securing
tiny knots
    The real occurrence is followed by the resting occurrence in
saying so

                The resting occurrence of shoreline cattle
                    complete
                Of sea complete
                Weariness (for you) was not that day
                    complete
                I think, it couldn't complete something
                    for you

                                        (LH)

Weariness suppressing the physical which is actually non-existent
then, though active weirdly, there seems no rest in one by its
contemplative place being suppressed.
    The resting occurrence could occur when the luminous
event's seen from the suppression of the physical state.
    Birds were seen above red grass in a dim blue from my
recession.

    Contrarily, (your) 'seeing the same' (of men securing the tiny
knots), and what's seen being 'always the same' is itself a physical
event, restful and luminous.

                                          (LS)

The conscious attempt to rest despite flashing (cerebral but mindless and stunning), to lose consciousness which would otherwise obliterate seeing (when what's to be seen constitutes what will become moving elements of memory), can't settle anywhere

Instead the flashing continues

Accumulating images — long houses in Brunei, the red veins of chard, the depressed town of Clear Lake, the fat fishing boy's sudden smile, an irascible child plunging into the supermarket freezer — glimmer in the cold light

These elements are active

Other images — icebergs, terns with pianos — are active but non-existent

I sometimes think of the poles — the arctic and the antarctic — enduring weariness

That's a private balance, seen in the brightness of the night

(LH)

There can't be conscious resting? There's only the physical state that's been suppressed which has become a luminous event one doesn't know.

It's one. That's the balance. Weariness is in the poles of the arctic and antarctic. The black sky with stars is in between.

It doesn't *occur* and is only a connection:

Billows of black clouds in strands raced across the red gel at one end of the sky. A hawk sailed in the huge racing strands without moving, with a tiny dog yapping a mile away under the flooding of the forming plate from the black strands.

Napping I dreamt the connection (of
it never being (connected) but couldn't
remember in the suppressed physical state

A separate sight:
There's red almost centipede
grass racing under this liquid
floating blue dim in the air
which is resting appearing not from seeing

19

from one's suppressed physical state
            moving
This isn't an event is purely
separate from the racket of people's activities,

(LS)

Moving back from the car at the end of the day in the red dusk,
        feeling separately racing (and tired), I consciously eye the
        grainy area dissolving
There's a glossy sky to the West
No surface sounds apply
I seem to be doing something in a wide perspective — but without
        idiosyncrasies removed
Thumb twitching, disregarding an amusing dog, claustrophobic
        from the smell of ivy, walking to the door
That seems to be the characteristic of occurring — idiosyncrasy
        and action

        Not quite in rest a dream occurs
        There's no gist to the man in the dream loving
        There's no history pertaining to the real man
        His image strikes
        He's a double, inactive
        He's mirrored, artless
        There's no distance
        Nothing like the vista in the action movie

(LH)

    After the spinal cord being operated on the other day, second
day waking, I was as if eighteen with only being elated existing seeing
the light come into the sky at dawn. The physical state can't end.
    Nothing like the vista in the action movie whose slight and
depressed plot producing action isn't an action in the day, which is
not quite in rest.
        Consciously looking at the dark roses. I went right
        up to them in the blue.

Dark red roses on a bush floated in the light blue — 'while' I was out walking.
The light blue isn't dreamed. The dark roses could be seen in it.

(LS)

In the flamboyant first moment of survival which you call a rose
           something in the world comes into sight
The efflorescing attention floats where the action will be
Future events (the recovery) are about to occur
Meanwhile the real eighteen year old waits to be recognized

Once there was a woman who drew what she saw in the dark. She was blinded. Sometimes she drew in milk, sometimes in lemon juice or indigo or blood or ink or egg whites and dye. In her left hand she held the cup and in her right the brush. The picture floats where the action is.

(LH)

The light blue whether dreamed or not doesn't exist — in seeing
           (I want to take it to that)
The occurrence being subject to that and only it (seeing) — is still 'one's life producing.' The recovery would be 'one's life still producing.'
        Whatever happens in life being irrelevant isn't 'seeing' the arbitrary occurrence of it yet.

        The adult seeing the serene life comes from the phenomena of conflict itself as early,
                   something in the world comes into sight
If we can't see the arbitrary occurrence of the adult's serene life — ever(?)
        as ordinary event the physical state, of the adult later, is
        endless
That's what happened.

(LS)

A demanding light blue production occurs after the night in which the adult draws in the dark. It challenges the independence of the figure I make, redrawn by invisibility in sleep.

My figure, isolated in self-scrutiny, is independent but can experience conflict, interrupt endlessness, and recover. I dream that a seductive man whom I alone know to be Hamlet is being detained at a border by customs and immigrations agents. I am now awake and will concoct a denouement. No one will arrest Hamlet.

All attention turns to Justice just as the blindfold is removed.

(LH)

It's receptive as solely dependent on one
(There was a study on the water leech's movement that took fifteen years)
'social' actions
seem to be what are events

I am now awake, so analysis is the elation itself, action being submitted to it
('from who's point of view?' — is itself the light blue)
One is the water buffalo not being felled in the morning; my effort is of trying to hit the rhino who afterwards enters one.

(LS)

In such watching we are setting to work
I wake to see the arrangement (or flotation) whose plenitude might be called 'light blue'
A play of sounds emitting birds
They are hits
But the arbitrary itself is boundless (which is why it is faultless — incorrigible)
The immigration agent in the dream represents the guard of boundaries
We can experience anything — but we don't, because we set to work (committed to a 'social' action)

The work precipitates birds — an organization of phantoms
    The action of phantoms (the stiffening of my position)
determines my sensations on hearing the birds which I can't see but
imagine to be yellow or scarlet
    One song is now obliterated by construction — "felled in the
morning"

(LH)

Actions is they're being sole *per se.*
That's just my scrutiny, so it's not existing.
The greyhound (has to be 'in' my ocular memory) ran 'over'
the yellow field which was dark. It doesn't have to exist in my
memory thus.
    The round bulb moon being far forward (not over the dog,
and behind me) floated then (: the border guard itself; the
immigration agent floats as one, and from any event being 'then').
Discouraged, I slip away (out of) from work from my being small.
    Being felled 'has to' be no order. A colon is that even.
    The light blue doesn't have weight on that dark. Or the dark
on it. A dream doesn't in it.
    Not working doesn't have any weight. Working sees it
though.
    A dream has greater weight than my activities when (one's)
washed over not existing at home. I just had one this morning. I
can't remember it, yet it being outside.
        where there's very little of me and of it

        there could be events on that line; it's not, however,
            suppressed
        that's the boundary guard, no suppression

        (Now I remember something of my dream someone
        was in love with me, not me to him I had as it
        happens to bathe in a toilet stall which was filthy
        which I tell him, he was going to bathe after and did,
        which I know is reciprocating your dream of Hamlet
        detained and the immigration agents, *per se,* that's
        mine's occurrence at all).

(LS)

23

Working begins
It makes things visible and then recognizable
It continues things
An interior

One's physical state puts one on the side away from the
        spectators
Or not 'opposes' but 'reverses'
Boundaries reverse
The wall at the work site reverses the spectators who are now on
        parade (on line)
(I agree with you that our consciousness is always being directed
        to *independent* active situations — they arise, arbitrary not
        in themselves, but exterior — not like dreams but
        acknowledged — in response to an ant you jump over the
        wall.)

                                                              (LH)

        The boundary guard being no suppression being in reverse it·
hasn't nature. It being in one's dream is calm as if floating in (outer)
        One's not subject to the boundary guard there in one's mind,
the same as 'there in existence'. (These are spatial approximations.)
        Work is that quiet floating up to contact

        The soft light grey in the cool is a quiet
        outside so it can be
        seen with one's mind, on
        a retina

                                                              (LS)

        (I remember your responding once, when someone had
asked how dreams might pertain to waking life, "Why would
anyone make a distinction between them?")

        On Tuesday in the evening light I see the wiggle of a tiny
moth with goal uncertain in flight
        Unexpected sights (pillars, banisters of light, forms along an

empty bridge, trees, a crowd) encountered at night in the thick grey
fog are finitely divisible into waking life
    Now (because I've said this) they are reversed
    I picture a street, feel dissatisfied with it, picture calm
pornography
    I seem to be watching the calm

(LH)

    I see the crowd of firemen enter as I'm back inside my
physical form receded floating in a rocking chair
    where I can see my own form by their noticing it as they run
by
    I'm in the dark at night there

    where they go by and that's in waking life, theirs there
which I see
    now I'm in waking life where it's not night

(LS)

    The firemen in black and carrying their bright gear join the
crowd of nearly naked marathon runners so numerous and, though
fast, serious and somnambulant that they haven't let the fire engine
through
    The bobbing runners carry the firemen along
    They are moving toward something quickly and dreamily
    Everything is formless except for a young woman who
thrusts her child in its stroller into the stream of runners and then
jerks it back
    With that vicious jab she asserts her right to be, in sight of
the blind runners

    Waking life cartoon events have marks on them

(LH)

    Intersecting in the stream of the firemen and the blind

---

runners, it's
        (there they're physical or one is to them)
        in the dark yet their waking stream
                where they're bobbing toward something quickly and
                        dreamily
        I don't see anything when I was just asleep

        the lights on the flanks as they're turning on top where they
ride, the strewn engines exhaust in the dark, several of them
        now they exhausted in the dark
        stretched out in (the naked crowd at) night

                                                    (LS)

        Your vividly saying the malfunctioning oven was pulsating
like a bomb in the dark surrounded by firemen streams into colors
and this attempt to see them and say so is my immediate and visual
response

        But I remember feeling upbraided when reading a comment
in a journal accusing "contemporary poetry" of being "optico-
centric"
        "It," said the author, "arrogantly privileges the eyes"
        "It," the essay continued, "colonizes the other senses"
        Yet I feel a sensation of light on the thighs — the strewing
that is emotion — stretching from my breathing in bed to a
helicopter at whose clatter I'm suffused with inappropriate
tranquillity now

                                                   (LH)

        One's on their thighs under choppers. The engines exhaust
the night beneath. The eyes float at night.
        Runners previously with amber intestines flit there.
Inappropriate tranquillity 'now' *is* tranquillity.

        At night they're the naked runners
        qualified by night rather than (by) seeing

                                                   (LS)

The nocturnal runners pass (congregations
        under the choppers) eyed by animals
        with unlimited range
The standard light gives only a slight lift
        to the solid flitting figures
While those who run without emotion are antisocial
        they are running in a human constellation
        (wolvish — but mothlike)
They have come to the run carrying very little
A yellow hardhat, a blue ... slat or wand
(I have to squint) ... or slide rule

In the background, the hour is late
Without my glasses, I'm at a disadvantage
Intimidated
An unblinking, changing phantom moves nonchalantly
        to this table

                                            (LH)

        I walked in a grey cool path (persimmons hung at the end
that's a cool grey light channel; it was an elating but clear, within
one, stream above flowing on the street). The persimmons seeming
heavy within it; they startled me because I came up to and finding
them.

        A flitting moth-person flaps in the black air and in the blue,
separating, seeming to ruffle, coming up to the dinner table and
beginning to wolf food.
        It runs up and is outside. That's just alive, barely. Whether
one's squinting and without glasses seeing it, one sees in the close
range
                the animals' eyes sailing on the black their being in it.
But the figures'
                and the animals' eyes sail (at) when clear blue too.
                One's physical being is elating there

                                            (LS)

27

Each elating statement (which increases the range of the senses) senses the animals' eyes, "sight overladen with the world seen"
We have an image of their lives in question
And of the violence of extremes

Then, physical, "I" enters the space I'm voluntarily examining — willful, therefore separate
I go along a street (on the shady side) and meet a man in a cafe who trains attack dogs
He demonstrates in a park that animals can change intention
His dogs, sailing at me snarling wildly, will land beside me smiling like pets

(LH)

Green exuding from the floating form,
from the rear their being old or sick having to not move, one (seen) shouting and not listening, is her having "sight overladen with the world seen," it seen at present.
The animals' eyes have that and one could, having that, move inside as not an imitation of one
glazed shouting occurs, her being glazed; recall tornado warning when I was bicycling in the corn and keep analyzing what's seen
so one's intention changes in (one's) flight, and could see any existence on the eyes
The gliding of the dog, a purple embroiled one (I saw a huge purple lunging one dragged into a laundry on a chain having been beaten to be that its only existence)
the physical being of the dog is elating there (making this comment about another being)
itself
purple flying embroiled, when it has been dragged before

so that the feet (now it's alert) float above, green exuding from its rear
one not listening could change the intention
to oneself — (!)
could be in movement without the intention — is, later

(LS)

_____

28

Seeing viscera (the invisible) as a medical student or as a
voyeur (then shadowed by an enormous coyote in the wild which
would remain visible separately uphill throughout) or an inspector
(this (world) at every moment sustaining the constant
development of opportunities for carrying out incipient acts (simple
motion)) taking the heart (with visible sensuality) in her shining
slate-pink hand
(the light as stone again)
with feet removed (the coyote continued for a mile
increasing intimacy)
the act (sight) isn't thwarted in its most direct path to
consummation
separating the curious parts from the blind angelic face

Without function (violence) or act

(LH)

the form of the visible coyote on a separate hill throughout as a
direct path

is dragged
in the dark
My yellow inflamed nerve up floating, 'in the night', so it's
'me', the eyes do float beads being outside not moved on the
recessed frame, which may walk.
The eyes don't seem attached on one's flapping cord waving
and reciprocate seeing.
The soft white lacquer flesh of the woman bathed on the
bed, an ocean, sprawled on it yelps as being sound in the lacquer
flesh only.
The soft lacquer holds only a yellow cord.
The visible coyote the same as the moon, moving on the
series of hills, they're within each other
the coyote's green emerald eyes on the outside
universe

(LS)

It is introspection that identifies one's place in the world as
physiological and not unique
            But it puts one in parts (object to a voyeur)
            And the voyeur itself is a part (a terrible face pressed
against the window from the outside and suddenly (though the
awful voyeur lingers) encountered)
            It has pathos but who cares?

            I remember a flasher in winter — it was 1954 among some
small trees
            He was irrelevant (because incomprehensible) and immobile
                        but (I think) it is the seeing that's existing
                        (in this social situation)
            However, the coyote (it was a guard) does exist unseen

                                                            (LH)

            like seeing through the slats of the train window the lotus
fields bogs with dark pigs in them
                        they come up arbitrarily, as they do in memory,
being seen — innocently appropriate each other's experience

            the notion of 'pathos,' *per se,* darkens intellect (which is the
same as pathos) is it the same as the guard?
            a darkened pig that lies lay on the emerald pad besotted by
the blue
            outside
                        The other night I was sleeping and lying by me in
            a hump of pillows and covers that were above me a man put
            his hand on me in them so that a mouse was running in a
dazzling   yellow
                        haystack in which we were lying, I screaming to him
            and (became) aware of it that it's a mouse while lying asleep
            in some bright day which is entirely
                        filled by this yellow haystack which 'appears' serene.

                                                            (LS)

Mice in the bed undertake the problem of a haystack
They leave it unguarded — this puts it 'outside', where it's
immobile and yellow
The nearly neon risen haystack quivers
Feeling a mouse without seeing it ('inside') makes
knowledge of its presence confessional
(but without enmity)
When someone confesses (when he or she "brings things out
into the open"), do you think it's the crime or the confessor "as he
or she is" (stripped of crime — unhanded) that we see
The woman 'arbitrarily' confessing that the man said,
"You've got to close her eyes"
'in the hay'

(LH)

Were a man to say as confessed to one "You've got to close
her eyes"
'in the haystack'
it is close to death anyway, because the risen haystack quivering in
an unnatural blue gaze obstructed or subsumed by the yellow isn't a
dream but a real occurrence in a state not-dreamed (though asleep)
There wasn't anything there but that. Outside pushed the
rungs.
as confession — enmity only in pain
so what's enmity or pain? One sees the physical body
has no end.
Theirs.
A mouse had been really in the haystack, run in a dazzling
hoop or arena.
The light wood flesh is dead when the yellow cord in it has
allowed it to be rigid. A wood figure floats with mouth.
I saw almost yellow almost nude shaved men lying with only
their imprints around them on walls, except for each other. They
would be curled or hanging in the air their rib cages like gills sacks
of delicate pouches.
One yellow man lying on the back of the gills extended only
the (powdered) stick arms and legs, so he's an infant — where
there's no thinking, only seeing so one flaps in this space with
emptiness, time for that in attention, even talking inside —

inattention of him being more a man from playing stuck on his gauze gill on the floor. (Sankai Juku. 'we're' seeing 'culture,' has occurrence inside only)

I wanted to cry being out because the wood flesh protruding on the sack played.

(LS)

There seems to be some story that is being left behind as the men stand out from their imprints
(a desert in sand "with great stillness")
never (unless meticulous mystics) abandoning their stories.
In a preserved story (perhaps a confession) people who are prisoners can tell what they saw
(not wanting to cry).
They stay with the story.
They sit in "new" yellow light on cold metal furniture, "lodged in hollows."

I was thinking of sex and of culture (both generating visibility) when I wrote of the mice "inside." Mice in "my" bed would brush not "my" entire body at once but places on it, its parts, and in doing so they would call "my" attention to them, disclosing their secrets: elbow, nipple, armpit, ribs, etc. — hence being on the inside they put the haystack on the outside. Its quiver is sexual, but outside, and therefore cultural. (I am speculating that anything linking inside to outside is "culture" — guards are such links, and so (I am proposing) are confessions.)

(LH)

The sack I saw (Sankai Juku) when playing it made me want to make a sound or had an opening of suppressed crying
The sack is in the burning rib cage (in my sense of it), as when one runs.
heaves burning in a cool air of evening. One's very small spatially.
I used to attack myself interiorially at age fourteen and had a

dream of a huge black dog trailing me through empty building and street, seeing the dog turn into myself, waking very quiet in myself, one's a boundary guard
       in a 'serene' way — to 'preserve one' is confessing itself — a link to ones 'as if' 'not in culture'
       It's seeing oneself as 'their' so enmity only in pain as if the moon's being forced to eliminate it and merely dilates and floats racing out
       one's eliminating the moon by the space of the night
       the haystack was an undreamed state, apprehended accidently — the mouse ran through a huge dazzling yellow space where I wasn't dreaming
       maybe the overwhelming yellow blotting an apparent blue, the yellow hay rippling not moving is 'by itself' 'with him'

                                                    (LS)

       When I went 'to work' today my hurrying there put a twist on the occasion.
       But now (it's late — 'old-fashioned') the (burlap) sack I imagine you seeing (loosely woven and porous) seems to have been a prop and a (closed or open) symbol
           perfected in being preserved
           and functioning.
       Such a sack — floral and grainy, like circus canvas — is a display (not a containment)
       but this displays grief (not anger) or frustration.
       The recalcitrant (immobilized) brevity (fixity) of being in (at) a perception
           (in which we're embedded, caught — *there!*) gives what we see meaning (*we* are lost).

       A search is undertaken and a witness comes forward and in this account a pleasant man has helped an old woman to her feet. A second witness says that an angry woman was flailing an old man with a cane. A third witness describes a belligerent couple, a young man with a cane and an older woman, demanding money (not of the young man but of the witness).
       And more witnesses fly forward. They all want to see (to have seen).

                                                    (LH)

see as being itself the objects (when one is walking)
which there doesn't make the deep red leaves descend raining
      so one has to see the descending rain in the heat of blood
red leaves in which the bicyclist tears
                — woman with cane decomposing in the red leaves —
red air with leaves
      events occurring are their chronology in the serial we're
                concocting only movements on a retina
            producing elation are outside, so one could just
            produce that elation as such in order to see what
            they are
(Spenser's *Fairie Queene* the prototype of the Classic comic
book, one scene after another only in a structure, there's no
difference between children and adults.
      There not being that essential change (as the worm to the
            black butterfly not able to be seen in the blue — as it
            is in night) is in *The Fairie Queene* already — that's
            the events themselves.
            Events are seen where they're not visible
there.
      To see them only where they're eliminated.

      he, while not speaking to me, or letting me speak, other
being present whom he sees as rank, speaks depreciating of my
'narrative' as being its nature *per se*
            as one does not appear to have rank
            that notion of narrative is 'how' it is seen, and from
which 'rebellion' is possible, and 'weak'; as being the depreciating
view of 'one'.
      mistaking the 'narrative' as singular — in being or mimicking
the culture, even in — rebellion (even when the 'narrative' is being in
or is 'about' rebellion — so for it to be of existence / of reality, it has
to be — in rebellion, here —

                                      (LS)

      A history of perception (composition), or of a single
perception (a woman in black gazes at the sea in the blue)
remaining but differing in memory over time, or of a single percept
(pure light glints on glossy green-brown swoop of water in fog) as

a phenomenon (a thousand suns) in itself rather than in an instance
of witnessing, or of an object of perception seen (but never 'caught')
by a series of perceivers — any of these might be a sphere rather
than a narrative, affixed to the sun's logic

(Being seen 'as a woman' divides one conspicuously which
is what threatens (from the outside) the physical body

The man is worried by *A True History* (by women) of
perception with no end which could be written in the
dark (to include a black butterfly).)

In a series of 'experiments' 'at a window' I am watching a
number of appearances which provide me with a biographical
sequence of experiences but may not among themselves appear to
have 'real' order. They seem 'arbitrary' to each other; a woman in
black being tugged after a blond dog on a long leash toward the
corner is not 'with' but 'in addition to' a meter maid in a loose
uniform tucking a parking ticket in a vivid green envelope under the
windshield wiper of a dusty red car; a heavy boy repeatedly riding
his skateboard at the curb in the parking lot and attempting to jump
it is not 'related to' the sikh in shirtsleeves lounging with a cigarette
in his fingers at the kitchen door of the unpopular Indian restaurant
across the street. But they are joined by an almost-invisible swift
but rational 'and' — a flowing conjunction, 'transitions in our moving
life' — which it is my goal to see
      with no end
      in the sun

as a quarrel to be dropped

                                    (LH)

I don't know if I can drop the quarrel — transitions and conjunctions
when ... seeing one's decomposing sack of flesh playfully and
calmly — 'Their' view is the actual world is symbolic and permanent
where a higher authority 'gives' meaning to 'scenes' (decomposing
having meaning)

so one has to be a nomad to

continually engage one's decomposing self
without 'meaning' and so actual in existence
'They' are (anyone), the heavy boy roiling

in the blue air on the skateboard
who are nomads who aren't people
in their reality
(when one who's alone sees and engages the nomads who aren't
people but look as if they are, only when they see one, these beings
pursue and drive the one who's alone mad carrying that person into
their nomadic realm — invisible to others who have not connected
with them. I saw this in a movie, so it films the non-human world in
them and one — one sees one in our own culture seeing the non-
human.)
There's a boundary guard but it is in social reality
or in a sole life

(LS)

The nomads 'who aren't people' are everyone ignoring
boundaries in moments of conjunction
They would dignify sentiment
Shifting among juxtapositions (connected by visible irony)
they (we) are postmodernists (feeling the way they (we) are seen)
Or, to put it another way, travelling is sentimental in that it
is inserted into emotional 'gaps'
Sentimentality ('a reconciling power' emphasizing
'paradoxes') here is coherent — conjunction would be impossible
otherwise — but as such it inhibits transition
I see this watching skateboarders again in the changing
twilight but thinking about the incremental 'plot' (moves — or
'removes') of Sterne's *Sentimental Journey* which turns each
momentary anecdote into the narrative equivalent of an aphorism
Aphorisms are united by the speechless pauses between
them
But travel writing is often sentimental in this sense: "The
first limit to disappear: the borders of the lips" (Jalal Toufic)
Real landscapes are united by such ironies (the moment
when Odysseus has himself bound to the mast so that he can listen
to the Sirens while unable to 'pass over' is a moment of definitive

sincerity
                — in this scene he has no authority)

                                                                    (LH)

        (other in) periods of time repeat experiences and 'discover'
(see) their 'incremental' forms
        which are (Skateboarders) (again) and (watching) them 'in'
(changing twilight) are all Sirens who (cling to nothing) (passing
over while seeing)

        Are moments of conjunction 'sentimentality' in the sense of
being a journey — travelling is incremental (essential) only (?)
        so if 'sentimentality' is reconciling (distinctions) and makes
coherent only by 'its' own emotion, being only its sole seeing, seeing
being distortion *per se* — relative (only specific distinctions as the
line of existing —) is transition
                the nomad has no authority
                who's in a sole life
the boundary guard has to not have a sole life then

                                                                    (LS)

        One's body cannot block one's thoughts or desires
        Therefore long, repeated, and careful preparations
(involving a prolonged or frequent picturing of events and a
meticulous anticipation of one's own participating) followed by a
period of patient waiting are necessary if one is to be or to receive a
traveller
        For the traveller tomorrow is not a new day but the same
day repeated at a distant place
        Repetitions sustain changes, increments of preparation, not
wasted but accumulated, the storing up of invisible improvements
that hold over

        A purely mental nomad (ghostly but having had no previous
life to be the spirit or shadow of) cannot commit the act of waiting
or preparing (cannot be)
        One passes one's desire right through it (unrecognized) (and

unsatisfied)
     It is not time but validity that passes (an expression
          — over the border)

(LH)

     The clamp of the back, convulsing, on its yellow cord —
(when out walking)
     the clamp of one closed on one — it can't open in the open
day, the thin blue lid of day in which one is waist deep.
     Walking in the tray (of the lidless air), the dark fiery jetting
trees are bursting in the thin cool.
     One's body cannot block the day in it which isn't even seen
floating.

     The hump closed in the open day is the nomad
          pure clairvoyant people open

(LS)

     At the corner of the building glowing in sunset is a silver
cart heaved onto its side with two wheels removed so the brackets
are gaping like open clamps. A man in a white coat is struggling
with the cart and says simply "stripped for parts." Then he says "by
those people." I want to say something but feel empty — as I do
when listening to callers on talk radio.
     The object in the sunset is empty but looming (easily
exaggerated) just as an ocular spasm in the dark coming out of
sleep (seen as a flat light) might be badly interpreted as one of my
own nomads ("those people") — what I am about to see — an omen
calling for contemporary dress (the norm: visibility, relevance, and
boundaries).

     According to the omen (a "portrait in miniature"):
          a border guard in a pink and yellow bonnet will take
me riding in an uncomfortable wire basket to an uninterpretable
location
          or
          a blindfolded border guard will stroke his lips and

regard that as (a yellow cord) proof of my vulnerability

(LH)

One's body cannot block one's thoughts or desires
as a luminous, by being repeated,
sight
the object in the sunset is empty
just one's capacity for sight remains still, in
being out on the street looking at the thick illumined tray
on grey at sunset — empty because
it's seen

while
subject to one seeing, it's how
it's seen; one's standing still
with the people moving underneath
at a corner

(LS)

In the dark (reversal) night interprets day
The "people moving underneath" are acknowledged in this erotic
      economy
I am taken by their moving thoughts and I go "over the border"
I see many sights in the light — which are later repeated in visions
      without nostalgia
But what if all their color were eliminated
One would wonder:
      a) is it merely not being shown?
      b) is something of the world stronger without it?
            bb) what might that be?
            bbb) and what is weaker — what is color?
                        — to what is it attached?
Tarkovsky says Antonioni forgot everything when he saw color
The colorful world consists of oblivion and pretty pictures

The epistemologist scratches at the red lump on her forehead. She
tells me that travellers must "creep" and "stalk." While she's talking

39

I am rubbing my fingers over the edges of the pages of a book.

On the way home at sunset I see a man in a blue shirt grab at a bug and catch it. He looks at the palm of his hand and seems surprised. Suddenly I see that a black and white dog has turned on him. It's ready to spring, its ears are pressed against its head, its lips are curled, teeth bared.

(LH)

Only in grey the tiny birds flit in the palm tree, one lighting on a fence and singing in the grey beneath — the dark interpreted day in (whatever's) being; not with color (there'd been nothing in sleep) where the pictures are not burned on the memory, so do occur in the vivid oblivion (but without it) one isn't united to the colorful world and in its oblivion. One is in heavy rain meeting people just outside, outdoors: there's only grey and therefore seeing them. Resting, they're burned in grey, at the time. At the post office mailing. Is death, and therefore knowing about memory, at the oblivion in colors which is people's movements — is their actions — the man in the blue shirt grabbing a bug at sunset, seen only at sunset, the blue shirt ruffles in the lit air

the blue shirt has existence by the hanging
bright persimmons in grey
many sights in light, in the colorful world
where one rests from merely existing. The light elation is the events in series.

(LS)

Oblivion takes the world in obverse. The colorful world there seen in negative is very colorful. Yellow plums fall into the red grass. There cannot be (in a world susceptible to oblivion) any distinction between inside and outside.

The works of oblivion hang like pictures at an exhibition in a museum abandoned by ghosts (memory).

In what country could that happen?

In my "memory" (torturously located) Spain appears (so it
is not a country abandoned by ghosts) — yellow. A sacred yellow —
dusty and nothing an artist could complete (it's incomplete —
infinite — in the sky, too).

I "catch sight" of a grey (unverified) lizard there. But it goes
into a separate fissure. Such shadows are very cold. I remember
that I sprawled as if I belonged in the interpreted sun — wanting to
be comprehended in a scene

(as an innocent)

oblivious, so that 'one' is not responsible for a romantic pleasure
(which would put one outside it) but is seen instead and sprawling

(stalking).

(The innocent is helpful, and the innocent is helpless, too.
The visible world doesn't get swept up for nothing.)

(LH)

There's no obverse as the moon freed in one floating

the colorful world is a paradise. Not to have any conception
of origin (in it) and the moon, still, free in oneself

yellow ghosts outside only in the red grass

men sulking in a room at a party had tiny 'souls' then that
were buds. The tiny rose buds wouldn't open

the world being susceptible to oblivion, the immense slab of
rose tinge of hurling cloud-continent rushing toward me (who's on
land), no moon in the sky — either outside or within the hurling slab
in the sky

would be leading the cow on the bright watery rivulets

(LS)

We would experience blindness head first (and as a
vulnerability, but of the world, too)

as moistness, breathing, or shore

(the obsolete word "bourne" comes to mind

and the figure of Lear).

41

The world sustains an infinity of borders and boundaries, overlapping outlines, interstices — zones
into which we are leading. We disturb everything — being helpful
and observant.
A cow is blowing in the cold.

Bright but colorless parallel horizons fill the vista when I close my eyes. 'Behind' closed eyes I have a sensation of 'seeing' panoramically, but the view is vertical — I see distance and surface before me from head to toe. There are no perspective lines. Or, rather, the radials extend but not from me. I am witnessing someone else's seeing — it's as if I were watching their perspective from the side.

(LH)

The head of the pink tulip, bunches of them fully open are blind — and aren't born; are eyeless and not born, or are born and are in fields where one cow is blowing
It moves in the fields whether it's disturbing them; they're not born and are existing anyway, it moves in them
They have this peaceful but wild existence — where everything's disturbed in it, but not by them
if the cow's behind it doesn't suffer and is observant, the tulips not being born (bourne) and being pink rushes

The Red Sea not to see filled with the violent pink rushes sustains the cow to have it wade, to have it walk.

(LS)

This doesn't feel at all like "looking back" over uncertain experience. Memories (in action) (and though retrospective) seem to face forward and move.
They (these) are communiques (chosen).
Things, one of consciousness and another just appearing, in a new place to which we have gone away.
We are looking at the town where "The Birds" was filmed —

42

on location it's incredible. But a terrific seabreeze is scattering the light. I have a sense of illusion, one in which everything is amusing but haunting (inexplicable). This is because I am an outsider.

In the film, the outsider (Tippi Hedren) becomes an insider under unnatural circumstances which, by the end of the film, have dazzled her so that she is outside again.

A local says that people from out of town always try to figure this out.

She tells us that the familiar yellow blossoming gorse clumps in the area are ineradicable invaders. They "come out of nowhere" like "ghost-born calves." She attributes this to forces. "The things we see," she says, "shouldn't be made to jump just for the sake of jumping."

(LH)

(The (ordinary) people going to a foreign country acted (became) greedy and cruel, because of the poverty and turmoil there.

They were made ferocious so they were made to be in the place of the Ancient Mariner — where they could not be blessed.)

(In the place where there were no goods: By oneself in order not to make any change in the people at the shopping dome so as to see them, lines formed apparently silently but with the hum in the glass tiered dome as if blind bumping while in the trail, with no motion.

From all lines I would be excluded, soundless, when I reached the front of the line.

Elbowed aside, there had been no movement before the one, when I reached the head.

I felt faint with hunger and entered a line in a compartment that was for repulsive weiners and sweet coffee. I wanted the coffee.

At the front of the line I held my arms like fins couldn't be ousted.

I was elbowed away from every surface then, where people stood, though there was space would bump me silent but with a hum as of hive creatures feeding hallowed halcyon coming up again to bump me from a surface where I'd come.

I would rest with the sweet coffee in the center.

It was calves feeding in water in the protected one.

43

I can't be blessed in the meanness of my own. The ghost-born calves as of whales bump me. There is only the inside.)

(Being away: Ghost-born are blessed and have no existing mothers (providers).
Tippi Hedren had come to Bodega Bay wanting to date a man whose mother's sexual jealousy wanting him manifested as birds. After being attacked by birds, Tippi Hedren falls into a daze stunned.)

(LS)

I think we see things fluttering in and out of narration. We expect (expectation here is nearly synonymous with greed) things to be participants (coerced, perhaps, by our willfulness) in our way of seeing. They "ordinarily" "speak" (mean) — i.e., things are logical, and according to that logic we see in fables.

The narration is the outside of seeing. It helps with identification (of a bird, e.g., as a "black-shouldered kite" hovering over the field in the pale morning light seen through binoculars across binocular latitudes several surfaces away (binoculars also flatten the leaves and branches of the bay tree on which we later saw an "osprey")).

Sir Francis Bacon says, "Experience when it offers itself is called *chance;* when it is sought after it is called *experience.*"

He continues: "Many objects in nature fit to throw light upon knowledge have been exposed to our view and discovered by means of long voyages and travels." (In a fable such a speech might be attributed to a kite or an osprey.)

From the mud along the creek in which the bay tree has its roots, a chorus of turtles might be given Bacon's comment, "We cannot approve of any mode of discovery without writing." (The mud was covered with the marks of the turtles.)

In a country without goods, marks would have been the (almost sufficient) substitute for them. By eloquently imagining visible and palpable things, the citizens could have sustained the plenitude of an inhabitable nation.

This simulacral (willed?) nation would have been a closed (self-defining) system. One might say it had been narrated into paradise.

Entering with a woman of such a nation into a milling crowd attracted by a rumor of sausage, then seeing a single man in a "lab coat" wheeling a cart of such sausages toward us, I was told that I didn't understand "such things," and I was pushed out of the crowd. The "grandmothers" and the "mothers" fought it out.

(You are right that the birds in "The Birds" represent, in their unnatural behavior, the possessive biological clutching of the hero's mother. Some (I haven't seen them all) of Spielberg's films (I'm thinking especially of "Jurassic Park") are also psycho-fables about the twisted relationship between parents (adults) and children, the incommensurability of their respective desires.

Laura Dern in "Jurassic Park" and Tippi Hedren in "The Birds" both play a "ditsy" blond outsider, a cute character (very manipulative) with bouncy self-conscious courage, who expresses the hero's sexual impotence (it's a bourgeois impotence, the fear of family), while taking the side (role) of the child.

Even the audience participates, witnessing the growing fearfulness of the familiar.)

(LH)

Ghost-born calves are from paradise, having no existing providers

Everything is fictional, so anything one says is dual narrating

Kogi Indians seeing: We live in a world shaped in spirit. Everything we do, any movement even, is an event not only in the material world but also in aluna (spirit world) which is intelligence, sensitivity, fertility. Making a film would be filming only the material world but in which the movements of the Kogi people, a hand gesture, is in aluna too. Their movements being in both can't be seen by the outsider (for whom the material realm is the only understanding, or foci, action); so the click of the camera's shutter injures the Kogi person participating. (The narration is the outside of seeing.) Sometimes movement is used by people to communicate from being in aluna rather than language.

Either 'experience' or 'narrating' would be dual.

hearing, or seeing, makes duration of phenomena

(LS)

45

The click catches a ghost, a veiled animal
There's no picture
The lovers, gesturing, in paradise are blind — nothing's
obscene — paradise is unbounded, abandoned
I turn to "see" (the term "ghost" is my only understanding of
that turn
                    meaning both "day" and "picture")
I take ten steps forward, making ten knocks on the floor

        Outside a group of gesturing men have crowded around a
fancy car which is programmed to defend itself: "You are too close
to the vehicle," it 'says': "Stand back!"
        The car "counts down" (10, 9, 8, etc.,) and begins to hoot
        The men are hearing the noisy comedy of their own
nearness — circling one thing
                            (it could be anything)

                                            (LH)

        The blazing blood-red trees are under a cement star (cement
structure of a Mormon temple risen on a pale blue horizon)
        one hangs by the car. crime waves are neutral in mirroring
crowds, are not sustained in or mirroring those of (the waves of)
breathing

        one breathing or crowds breathe in the blue

                                            (LS)

Someone looks at my eyes but not into them
I'm inspected
Actually, I suspect myself
Self-consciously I read that "sometimes he looked at my nose,
        sometimes at my chin, then straight at my eyes again"
The mirror bounces on the crime wave, jerking the sky

But *this* conscious seeing motivates conscientious observing
The nervous responsibility to worry about crime won't distract me
        (I vow) from my thorough thrilled look at the sky — clouds

Clouds "look like" means we read in them, relaxed
The "witches" there are not "criminals"
No form is visibly criminal
A space of light without clouds exactly replicates the neck and
      head of a turtle peering

(LH)

    Blood-red, a wave sustains no crime wave
    to inspect by looking at the eyes but not being in them
    the neck taken out oars
    (that are a crow) in thin blue

    the subjective movement of the neck, a wave breathing in
blue, the turtle coughing black but breathing finning in the endless
wide air also
    inquisitive gets cut off an oar singly

(LS)

    A photograph is taken in the dark
    The photograph is taken into a woman's eye through a hole
and it shows a blood-red and yellow circle of mind
    In the photograph the mind is framed by the emptiness in
the eye
    But the eye seems to be looking out
    It is specific (personal) and yet behind nothing
    It looks, too, like a yolk
    It lacks neck
    It is intimate (finite) but unflickering — but there can't be a
picture of that, only an interpretation, an empathy
    The eye is the eye of its own accord

    But she who sees is herself seen
    This is not a static melodrama but an inquisition, leaving
desire hidden (finning in the endless wide air)

(LH)

robins hammering in mass advancing on the lighted green at
evening hopping if one / hammering is at instant of lighted evening
— light little herd outside / only (is that)

the physically blind don't miss as there are their absences — there is
their absence

(LS)

All bodies then — living and dead, clothed and naked, human and
      bird — share the spectators themselves forming spectacles
At the edge of the spectacle is the tree
A near nude disturbed in a taut hammock (she is wearing only a
      belt of feathers) sees a man (who is Amerigo Vespucci)
      advancing
The tongue of the blind, an anteater on the ground, is extended
      — licking
That is the general rule — flickering

There's an inflammation, as of robins, between them (male and
      female)

(LH)

There's an inflammation, an iris, between them

Amerigo Vespucci couples a deer. Collaboration is calm.
    The flickering tongue of the blind woman on the visible Red
Sea, the water's red, is in the visual reality — for her.
    The flaps of the iris are in her within blind flicking her
tongue outside.
    Some are naked as in being ferried on Lethe and an iris is
between them here and there now in the water.

(LS)

From the bottom of a lake a deer rises
It's night

48

It opens the lake through the water (which is quiet in ebony cups)

Through the opening the men in the lake smell the land
It spreads itself out (so they "discover" (desire) it)
The deer is in sight
In every version of the story the men rush out through the opening onto the land after the deer
The land there is disquieting
One man (who is Daniel Boone — holding a torch) shoots the deer and marries it
Daniel Boone catches sight of the eyes alone but knows the whole deer

 Other people at dawn
   in the dark
 They are out
   in shock

(LH)

One hasn't 'known', can know, the partner physically and the earthquake being prior doesn't cause this event
One isn't a child from devastation but is so first, as such. Having married the deer (one) emerges from the iris is free when having been born.

Don't put that under any observation which (isn't before), though marriage with the deer is. The houses in the area are blasted apart, thunderbolts (after the fissure). People wander arising or from the quake (only; how could it be only?).

(LS)

Arkadii Dragomoshchenko writes that events are a form of co-existence (he can say this in a single word, since in Russian *event (sobytie)* can be divided into the prefix *so (with* or *co-)* and the noun *bytie (existence* or *being)*). What holds us to our events might be not threadlike but cloudlike (and always contradictory). The very obscurity into which the woman from Cambodia, blind now, looks may be the brutal events that the author of the article about her says she does not, *cannot,* bear to see — or, rather, what she sees now is their relation to her. Hers and their coexistence.

She and what she sees are simultaneous. But what she sees is what she saw, so she lacks loss. She is deprived of grief and of relief.

She is completely deprived of a void and its clarity and blue.

In an emotional cloud, no comparisons are possible. Coexistence is true of its own accord.

(LH)

Herself and the sights co-exist. This is 'age' also. Supposing the sights either beautiful or frightening co-exist with one, one's dreams move — ? (Or don't so one is near death-saturation. Maybe they move heavily in her. or she doesn't see them?)

We're not to see events in the same constellation.
Reading Jalal Toufic's *Distracted,* my attention flitting constantly, but *to* the edges or flickers that (are to) occur at the same time in any place of it, and not diverted to something else outside it except *occasionally,* my distraction became itself *per se.* This is interesting in being 'without' 'content' (or 'contentment') so that it tries to impinge again.

As if dream-deprived. with 'contentment' and depression in that.

(LS)

When I see nothing, I am only guessing
Or dreaming
Sight is lyrical, because its subtext is annihilation
The descriptions (witnessings) (then), which are of co-existence,
    'age,' contain both aphorisms and saturations, although this
    seems contradictory
The interrupted continuing, seeing and blind

I see a man walking two gazelles, beautiful disfigurations of
    someone he loves
Memory here misunderstands, afraid of leaving anything obscure
They are overlappings, from his point of view, when he is not
    suffering from uncertainty

                                                                    (LH)

        Disturbed by abandonment,
        by someone who is not the same person, (who) seen again,
before me maintaining the dissimilarity of their actions to the
appearance (to me) of these actions — I chose without remembering
these to see two movies in one evening, *Bullitt* and *Vertigo.*
        Placed beside each other, without remembering, their plots
were the same. In both, a person who is to be protected is
apparently killed so that the protector (oneself) has failed; yet
someone else has been substituted and dies for the 'real' person —
yet is then that 'real' person, in *Vertigo,* irreplaceable not found again
even when alive.
        Found again, in both, the real person then actually dies —
so that one has failed again, and is left without access to 'the
one'/'the same person', who does not exist (ever). (In *Bullitt,* the
'real' person, having first substituted another, dying, can't then be a
witness, but not ever intending to be, isn't *ever* a witness, as
possibility.) The subtext is annihilation, walking two gazelles (the
one one loves) both disfigurations of 'someone he loves' —
        as the main text is abandonment, which is love.
        Choosing (without remembering the plot of) the two movies
at that moment was the similarity of the people's actions to (the
actions') appearances. Seeing appearances in one's own mind by
forgetting is a very simple ("lyrical") way.

                                                                    (LS)

        Fitting actions to appearances is literal, the dilemma
matched to description so that it is visible
        I watch for the stand in or stunt man brought on because
he's prepared for what's coming
        But the substitution may take place under his feet, as when

                              51

Gloucester is brought to the edge of a ditch or conduit, itself the discrepancy along which intelligence can pass

The appearance is kept but the act is effaced, so that the old man remains safe

The substitution of one for another is not like the lyrical replacement that occurs when one is aging

In the film, youths are singing as if walking animals

"I want to see you again," they say

But "you" cannot direct the love another feels toward you

(LH)

not abandonment

The rib cage floating in the shock occurs later, not chronologically — so that concentrating one *at first* chooses a moon bounding floating — in sheets of pouring rain, as that occurs. A man clothed in black in the black, sneaking as feet placed side-by-side, like a big fox carrying a stick that floats out horizontal on his shoulder (dragged behind) with his wild eyeballs seen — our (my) wild eyeballs catch in the black

We're running outside tearing after him like bats on the boards a line — in bare feet by torrents of pouring snow in the sky — rather than the moon as chosen bounding. As one's sole movement's

(LS)

We realize that *this* is the moment. It is only *now* that the place we're in (the geographical site) and this particular wind and cold (winter) are coinciding perfectly to produce the swift and vivid whirlpool we see plunging in the turbulent milkblue stream in the snow. We see a dog, its mouth open to emit a branch, whose swirling leaves the wind tosses and the snow covers with the shapes of whores in a bawdy tavern under yellow lamplight. Hundreds of suns the size of coins swirl in the whirlpool and are sucked into the snow — the snow has consumed thousands of such images

avenged

inefficiently avenged by dream images
but out of place
the best ghosts we can devise
usually running, pulled
divided from the persons they would haunt

(LH)

The starving ghosts. Thinkers looking at them, when they were in hell, reprimanded the society that 'spawned' them; yet considered it more kindly when the starving bags running out to be fed — who can't receive calm, in different run-on scenes (so they're 'official', visual-social, in 'fact') in their continual single lives — were quieted.

they desire, are in greed — not the silk black irises. I sewed them, in the black — outside — before dawn.

thinkers disapprove of torture, even if we're tortured in fact as the physical body *per se.*

the fragrant prince, warm man as the physical body, bitten by the tsetse fly, lies down saying I've been bitten by a tsetse fly, and sleeps, exuding perfume. He is contemplation for one.

another day, (day itself magnolia bud — clad rose-flesh as only the day *per se* (which is inside the eyes) — yet when it's past dawn. it isn't moving. but black (before, another day) was voluptuous.) thin air, seeing rungs of magnolia cups, buds. (that's the only difference from sleep).

I wasn't avenged by the dream images, though they were troubling — I awoke completely peaceful and began to be riled/aggressive only by the day (without images but the buds...no content).

(LS)

No content — it's as if the last residuum of visibility — not merely the last thing seen but the last quality adhering to it that allowed it to be seen — its sphericity, perhaps, or glossy knobbiness or reservoir of color — had been isolated in a cabinet of monstrosities in a quiet, undisturbed, imageless, unmemorable universe. Visibility, diminished to this one but outstanding thing, would no longer fill each day. The fullness of the invisible world would be like that between window panes at night or under the ear pressed into the pillow. The last visible thing would be incomparable — unique, unnameable, undreamable.

> In medicine visibility cannot be taken for granted
> Each body conceals a person revelling behind
> persistent moonface
> Its few deep displayed lesions are melancholic — and
> an imposition
> Everything hopes to be shown
> Each skull celebrates the moment at which an
> invisible hand writes across its cranial suture
> And the resulting illustrative sequence known as
> "the sliced face" mocks the serenity usually
> achieved when a thing matches its name
> Or when generosity noses the tight spot between
> the eyes

(LH)

insufficiently avenged by dream images implying a relation to one that's imageless while only visible
as walking lost in the gutted area by drug dealer throttling another man saying he'd kill him, standing flagging while drug dealers speak into the panels of phones on the street by one a taxi low swimming in waves.

Not 'avenged' sitting in the fashionable bar but a context where anyone could not be afraid and anyone would simply be afraid in the other context.
The notion of being diminished undisturbed as the residuum of visibility, which no longer is 'in' the day that is its residuum of visibility — as serenity where 'one' isn't disturbed, by not existing isn't contrary.
Language is simply some other location or a diminished residuum, unnameable, not illustrative of the other. One recognizes it then as a serene visibility,
in one, whereas I'd thought only visibility was that.

(LS)

54

We are citing what's seen, mobile and mutable details taking part
      in a greater drama of visibility
There is serenity in the greater drama, little in each sight
And that's argumentative — as is irony, sentimentally extended over
      the gap (residuum) between what can be seen and what can
      be known
The argument makes a deal and achieves something — what is
      visible in the light will remain (half-right) and what is
      invisible will vanish (half-right too)
That explains both "moonface" and "sliced face"
So does the image evoked by the terms "profile" and
      "discontinuity" and "film"

Just this past Sunday I saw a film — its theme was "blind loyalty"
The emotion was sustained by thought, not visibility
By the time the hero became aware of what he had (or had not)
      seen, he was too old for revenge

                                                (LH)

'emotion' as motion of events which are occurrence so that it is
      a movement in (horizontal) 'history'
therefore serenity can be seen throughout —
      serenity as the 'structure'
      (which *is* the structure) is a residuum — then

we're sustained by serenity
      not in one's thought (outside maybe) (one sustained by one's
thought) where one didn't even have a memory of it —
blind memory having a weight, counting (being) in time — spring (?)
— as the
      slight weight of spring, is

                                                (LS)

      Emotions are like spring
            — recurrences
      The universe is horizontal
            — again

But here's an unseen situation — I feel an emotion and I'm keeping it free of the characteristics which would make it comparable to a thing (with a thing's motion and visibility). It's not momentary, but it is more like time than material. It's unimaginable — uncontained, in that sense — but it seems nonetheless palpable and animal.

It provokes no image of itself.

The word "again" would be pessimistic in this context — because the recurring feeling of the emotion is aimless, it has no goal.

The blinding horizon stands in the way

And why not something next, decentered — ?

Horizon, dispensation, a pass on the far side of the focal point

(LH)

— yet warped is an imitation of the interior of an event even.

Then one's decentered throughout. So suspense is a thing. It changes the relation of phenomena. Corpses enflame the mind — where crowds are seen eating pears. No structure inhibiting existence.

Being alone is in the enflamed or quiet mind merely — apologizing afterward to another and sitting eating a pear.

(LS)

The larger the crowd, the more distant it must be and the smaller the figures in it, if one's crowded out. On the other hand, the crowd might encompass engaging golden age populousness. Members would be drawn to the honey, where others are waiting or talking.

An expert (in a popular game requiring strength) has been hired to talk in the crowd (as soon as he has their attention) and apologizes — despite his abundance of actual experience.

His disclaimers bind one to him. The crowd disperses and regroups.

He is vulnerable. That puts him in power.

In excess, one feels crowded in.

(LH)

Being vulnerable and therefore in power is a criticism *per se* and description (outside) of someone — not in the crowd — then — obstinate and stubborn and without any power.

As this — then — very hardened person utterly without power apologizes to someone in the crowd, a ball flies from a game that's going on somewhere, the characteristic of which is of no one being bound to anyone, in the crowd having strayed from it.

The ball straying in the golden age populousness — not an inner occurrence, or it is but as something else — appears to float toward (Benjamin's angel) the viewer in an arc above the only location, which is the present
— if suffering had no other characteristic as vulnerability or stubbornness and is change it's visible?

(LS)

An interior reflection ...

[Cumulative and mutable, it's the boundless reflection of "broad daylight."
"Life has to be taken seriously —
Things change when they land in a book."]

... of an ordinary action.

(LH)

Wet, not seeming so, maybe it is not, perhaps Dante. The pale white face tunneling runs through the bright air, with the enflamed trees, that having shot up 'before' early, can burn as only color in the thin cobalt whereas the hole-eyed rat-face tunneling as if face on a heavy barrel is of a 'younger nature' rather than a white paste no-corpse in the cobalt but which has aged outside (in which you can see it having aged before but it is in the present).

The rat-face white sweating its limbs not even visible tunnels in the flaming cool air, toward one.
It has no place or interior life. There is no reflection in the place. But there appears to be a boundless reflection in that around or along with it.

(LS)

The notion "going to the dead" is very pure — no image should be attached to it

Mammals, meanwhile, appear when one is relaxed
When one is relaxed "there" is neither "that" nor "this"

(LH)

never being derided so one could not stand any negative occurrence there is no inner dusk?
they appear with each other, ghosts, the other first time, in vast cloud that's on the entire rain.
meeting — leader swinging toward me to be over me, but there was a gap in the branches, dropping a stream of dung to me — alone, I was embarrassed at having angered them — and their feeling that was weakness — while they screamed derision at my walking quietly.
is embarrassment originated in contact? different from saying embarrassment is social, contact of dusk?

(LS)

We are in a predicament: we are in a foreign country (I don't know where) and we are in theory.
The only other figure is in an empty place and no one is in the figure.
To reach this neighbor and its neighborhood I must act in

defiance (casting the bit).

Meanwhile, they say there's going to be a black-white morning ('denarrativized by the art of describing') to wake up to. Yesterday two wolves loped over it; all hunters have been warned off — Memory's daughters must be made happy at home.

(LH)

Freeze — die — come to life, a white-grey sleeting mud landscape of only people — in hovels — except a pig kept in bed (as it will freeze otherwise) where it skitters over people appearing to have been coupling with them (a woman and a boy) seen skittering 'after' (the coupling, which is only to the viewer 'outside')

a boy, a child (childish here is destructive) — some people understand things though — all motions are coming from single 'places' or 'views' — a man — from the 'Jap' camp — burning, having set himself aflame?, in the snow — are on the consciousness of the obtuse childish vibrant (adults the same therefore) (we, the viewer, may interpret later — the camp of the burning man is of war prisoners? but there is no historical time given to anywhere, the boy 'inside' either does not know the circumstance/reason of the burning man, nor 'consider' it 'think' it to the viewer so that it exists) mere eggshell who does pranks still. Yet as if he's an adult while a child. None, nothing, even no future, people in prison, of the boy's people also: everyone is throughout (which exhilarates the recipient viewer).
(Its being a constructed series of events — in which nonetheless the viewer, not constructing by being a viewer [outside], is the same as the people of entirely other circumstance in it — only heightens the intensity, not lessens by seeing it. Because the viewer recognizes the accelerated dismal bliss which is *the grungy and viewing per se* as real?)

(LS)

Hasty clairvoyance seems to come from unguarded childish memories —

59

That is, the prelude to extreme acts (which proscribe the future) is haste —

Haste here is not a sprint through time but an extended moment of attack —

Attack is the temporality of haste —

Haste occurs at the moment before a murder —

It occurs because the person about to commit the crime cannot stand surprise —

The criminal becomes the recipient of haste —

An immolation? The old snow is pitted where the accumulation has fallen off the trees; it's tracked up by animals (the deer are dragging their feet, the elk have been pawing at what looks like ground-growing mistletoe). The pressure is dropping, everyone wants to avoid surprise by going to sleep. I too have been making less of everything.

But I wanted to comment on metaphor. The thing for which a metaphor stands is in return that metaphor's metaphor. The images mirror each other, back and forth, but, as the number of reflected images increases, instead of getting smaller and receding, being metaphors, they get larger.

(LH)

One, told to, rolls over and on the left side a sharp disseminating flesh pain unfolds in one, and is seen (SPLAT — like the comic books) as the coagulation of an accumulating blue pool that's on that side.

One sees where sight can't occur, or memory? (The comic books are memory.)

The blue pool has entered the face, the cheek and left side of the head, and the pinned left leg fluttering in muscular-pain as if upright walking? Yet though being seen by others at the time (who are taking pictures), it is only seen by the one in an inner accelerated sight — blue — at the moment of the blue falling into the head. Flowing, rather, perhaps slowly.

(Criminal of haste, the burning man — him also a 'criminal,' prisoner in camp?: having created a sight — but 'historically' separate from one who's the viewer outside — though it is temporally collapsed)

The temporality of haste, movement of sprinting while quiet — having learned to breathe as accelerated motion at all times, in the upper chest only, as if running always — the other chambers are frozen and reawakened (can be only without the condition of sprinting while quiet — only quiet)

can indicate the earlier spatial configuration in the mind's remnant which is 'its' conception of it after it has occurred — its physical existence, unseen.

The sun took only a minute to change position into the eye. Water had no taste.

(LS)

The humiliation of the senses inverts memory into surfeit (such that resistance blossoms into collapse and collapse becomes a harbor of sorcery). Each image of the comic book is that collapse, "the second part of the sizzling erotic classic." In the last collapse the naked man has plunged into the naked man in the naked "Emmanuele": "We're different, uh? Ha, ha, ha!"

"What a beautiful smile!"

The affability of the supplicant ("that soft ball over the flame") results in a collapse of one eye, not pictured but mirrored — the comic book is a hall of mirrors. The "sorcery" is not an exercise of obscenity but an exercise of resistance, which immobilizes (frames) it (out of memory).

There is no storyteller for it. It can't be remembered because it has never happened before. Therefore it can't be understood.

(LH)

Hawk living on voles whose population dying from epidemics might fall by 90 percent at times, the hawks maintain themselves on the few voles then for the voles drop urine on their trails, marking, the urine being neon in ultra violet light in which the hawks see. Looking down on the land the hawks see the urine trails in ultra violet.

The senses expanded to inner seeing in ultra violet —

without inhibition or surfeit, and inhibition itself inner seeing then:

breathing only in the upper chest throughout life as if one is running responding always, even without one's movement — produces sense of accelerated seeing, while the deep lower chamber with no breath in it is motionless. Breathing in the frozen chamber first — illusion occurring of the hawk floating also — one sees without the faculties of sight *per se* in a range behind one of vast black land.

Other senses are created and learn there; the ultra violet light which the hawks see is there, the night being there hanging with black irises at the same time:

THUD — in the written comic book — but when, without reading, the person is dumped on their side, later. Then a blue pool formed along the side on which they were dumped, in the left leg and left side of head, which they saw within.

The man comes up and puts his part into the black lips of the iris hanging in the ultra violet — sort of reality reversed itself — so he sees the neon black iris illumined inside in the ultra violet sky.

(LS)

The waking images (of information) are, I think, learned
The features of those images (through which we gain access) are augmented (taught) until they are capable of accelerating orientation — our orientation toward experience

So when I want to know what a dog (let's say) is like, I open the comic book, in which the paw of a languid long dog is pressed against the frame keeping the dog from us (our part), its fixed seething tongue epitomizing a gooseneck reading lamp dramatically stereotyped over a cluster of observations

We want to know the power of this on our part — an externally directed (turned on) action drawn like a blind (insight) inside the space made for it by the boundless blue winter sun which is unparted, "like that of a train in the distance," its light flashing (after all) into the part

(At a bushy crossing, toward dark)

With a figure darting to the right (our eyes follow) and then, as if adjusting to signalled information, hurrying instead to the left

We all participate in this, receiving visual education

(LH)

(our present age which is in early childhood); and moves
backward as surface into a black land in which we are much older —
are ourselves, whatever that is. The dog reaching with its paw and
pressing our part then is licking — where the voluptuous lips of the
black iris hangs in ultra violet light, the past occurring being as
adults.

Yet makes an imagery, but in which the seething tongue is
vast entering the space of the opened black landscape.

The folds of the black irises in it flutter, the dog running
through them.

Man-eating tigers that leap from the waves to drag people
from boats — descending into the waves again, following people in
the forests do not attack when people wear masks looking
backward. Until the tigers learn the masks were images, only
appearing to be looking, as if not waking. They resume attacking
and eating the people.

If there were live eyes on the backs of our heads we would
be animated back in the black land, a blue winter sun rising, and our
not being attacked.

A withdrawn, whining father not wanting work and a
vicious doctor agree in the hall that the father's baby girl with the
sewn end-to-end operated-head opened merely learned in the
hospital to want attention, rather than that something occurred
there; which is backward as if there were some reason not to give
her attention.

The baby who is seeking (derived — ? — from occurrence) is
in the present light where the doctor is emanating streams of anger.
So the baby as an adult is back in the ultra violet light bearing vast
black lips in her middle.

The dog comes to her lapping with the tongue.

(LS)

The wakeful are embarrassed by the (embrace of) sleeping

63

As thumb in its important blue pressing flutter (giving ourselves attention) we must derive

(LH)

Formerly only breathing thinly, accelerated seeing that's not from the eyes (or going into the eyes from outside) was in the chest.

At present being in early childhood. Pictures, as verbal only, are simple — one in the past only as an adult, from the same one being a child as the present, plowing in the pampas grass.

As one is breathing as if running (and is running, plowing in the grass) yet the breath in the formerly sealed thorax chamber that is as if resting in quiet, the blue bulb of sun just rising, is also in vast sheaths of white pampas plumes that are swept between the one person's legs.

Someone can anticipate someone else's experience yet reverse it into a false or rather neutralized present — visual is only distortion, the event occurs experienced.

Here the adult cretin, in reference to the other — had put his fingers in another man's gel which he'd (the cretin'd) opened, a blue pure sun bobbing.

(LS)

The baby was held (like a dog which is like a thumb) up out of the grass and into the blue light of the sun (a freeze)

This (holding up like a thumb) reoccurs at the middle, but in mimicry (therefore dependent), which is only *like* likeness, being without beginning; it is always only returning

The claiming and reclaiming that occurs empathetically is a captioned form of propriety, as in: "Uh oh! Here's our little living threat to public decency!"

In the comic book the figure (like a novelist) is isolated "in the garden of the Renaissance man," uncounseled and unable to counsel others.

In the comic book, Homer is dreamless

One's middle (an upheld baby) must be excited, associated
— so as to be removed from humiliation
That of bobbing, being blue

(LH)

— so that wakes disoriented anyway utterly relaxed — no
one

no breath in the thorax, and then a dead relative (that being
recognized) — one begins to weep and laugh at the same time — as
inner thorax not breathing — opening on the span of bridge —
someone else — at a meeting — asphyxiating blue — is
hugged by two jumping up as the cure to asphyxiating — not
dreaming —
in my deep sleep — so that I can't resume a structure — out
in the car going out but am casting for it — the thorax not breathing
still, even in the prior sleep

(LS)

There was naked news of the death transmitted — not a
phrase (every phrase is linked to other phrases while the
information of this death lacked links) but a byte that repeated
(fetishized) the information — it stopped
Telegraphed
Captured
"Too simple," says the woman (sliding forward on her
leather skirt) on the brass bed (a baby elephant is standing on a
pedestal with its feet delicately drawn together like the stems of
four flowers in a bouquet)
"I'd rather be nude"

There's been a gentle exchange of bodies
A young male (I couldn't sleep) steps away from the bed
provoking (sharing) our grief with a death he reads about

(LH)

woman motorcyclist a black bumble bee in the blue —
if the event is the rim of one body's perceived field — the
blue sun freezing rose — then one has lost the controlling structure
ahead (the blossoms open, and one isn't 'that')

So transcription in cells is the magnolia buds flaming
upward — ahead, in one's sleep. Is there social experience a
separation occurring — ? at all

Whoopi, then. There's a gentle exchange of bodies there —
even to the dead

(LS)

The concentrating experience of the "gentle exchange" (we
lost our organs to each other) draws on three of the terms
(introspection, intuition, and interpretation) fundamental to the
experience of phrasing it

Outside of a numb frame

Amazed (neither forward nor backward) and without fetish
— though that which means the real organ may not actually be it

Is the woman motorcyclist in blue leather? an organic V?

As an emblem of birdlife, imprisonment

I was told of (and so I visualized) a prison whistle blower
himself telling of the birds' sexual world

The whistle blower saying "I should know" because "I was
one of them" required to "suck anyone"

In a numb frame

Renamed
Yeah!
The history of the moral sense is not quite long
The blue slides from the comic book deixis into action

(LH)

It's (also) the opposite — the bumble bee in black leather
made unreal by the woman motorcyclist — itself —
as if there weren't frames in the blue — our eyes are slides

themselves — but the black bumble bee is both still and moving — out — on the span of the bridge — seen (or not?)

another woman waiting at the end — people dream objects, as being not only those objects *per se* but socially their dialectical thinking occurring together — not far back, as the dreams — ?

(LS)

Just as the dreams come forward like lizards in the harbor (they are very chatty and treading water which three times rises and falls), each memory of them, however detailed and interpretative, bobs into the momentary (refusing fixity) and negative (denying the world what it wants)
So as to be in view, sustained by a sculptural effect (weight and plasticity) which is essential to the dialectical occurrence, objects under observation, woman waiting for woman, child petting a dog-faced lizard-tailed soft tall red pet kangaroo

There was an old man who'd "gone bush" in order to stay "in motion" at the prison, a red cemetery, the plastic flowers on the graves exploding in the heat (a rubber doll on a child's grave had gone black, unconsumed)
Relating to many things which had previously been undreamt of, simply opposite

(LH)

— where there are birds, or flowers, on black —
(wild/flowering)

horns begin — lift off — after (only) apprehension, motion — of people
crowd flocking to death — photographers sticking cameras in the faces as they bow as clear in them, not worshipping — (is not outside of viewing) — which the journalists are mocking as such (in their motion, then)

the figures (that: are in death) shouting, leaping making
cries — catching those fleeing, yet lightly — as the crowd's flocking
in to that, panic motion, to reach it — the ones mocking viewing are
in it merely — too.

(LS)

The visibility of something is never the detail through which
it resembles something else. But in visibility, as in leaping,
mumbling, worshipping, mocking (*"per se"*) something more than
ontological self-sufficiency is established. The imagination is
invoked and images transpire, and in each of them a (spectral)
history hovers — a counterfeit *per se*. Or counter-fact. The cameras
in the faces are allowed to be overly interpretative.

The woman on a motorcycle is on a span. Visibility is such a
span, and "a woman," being notoriously made visible "in span,"
might actually make use of her (invisibility) secret mobility. Such
(waiting) invisibility (fleeing) flowers. Is the panic there over-
interpreted — there *per se*?

(LH)

panic — in *me* — seeing. it's in the rush of those flocking in
(visibility of something the detail through which it resembles
something else, that) — that's in the cry made from the whole
verging pushing on the circle, shouting figures calling leaping
running — with animal heads, projections of 'one' 'speaking' or
apprehension — a crowd as one's (resistance is external 'only') — it
isn't the figures, but one's — flocking — only [in Bhutan where I was
traveling]
the figures are light joking — to bring — which makes the
separation floating

as bringing/going is halcyon. so
interpretation isn't — one — rush (can't negate — at all) — of
interior — that's them — only.
the part on death. motion of crowd not seen — is —
one — external only as desperate in one 'seeing' but as only the

68

factual motion. *as* one. their. it's motion, that is (of panic) to get there.

(LS)

The sight occurs in stages, separating thoughts
A thought (as event) draws the crowd in which it conceals
itself
A driver brakes within shouting distance of a man ill at ease
as if in a fiction which no one can negate — a cowboy or cop fiction
I, like everyone else, can't foresee what will happen — not
even what I myself will do
The cop points in outrage at the sun and then at the crowd
as if causation (interpretation) were his
Flailing
And then he is forced off, without the crowd's having any
thought of interpretation, between red cars — and is lost among the
many flirts flocking (into visibility)

I (pinned down) want to avoid the point at which the
(circling) joke "turns ugly" — bare and indelicate
But I want to know what's happening
And since such knowledge is always situated, I don't run off

(LH)

Is secret mobility — existing here — rather — than the
photographers being their visibility, their not included — are —
negating experience(.) — they'd simply be there without it,
before apprehension, they're never having any — bombs planted that
take people away; people bathing in canals in garbage not being
regarded somehow as experience (or experiencing), nor panic
arising from wanting to come to it, rather the minute seeing of 'one'
being 'flocking' as being 'them' is that which can be seen only as
negating
it(self)?

So minute mobility has to be separate — to be — 'our' —
('cognition' is films, say) — but our existing anyway, that it separates
outside of interpretation — ? — and could also be (is) seeing the

69

people in canals, who are sold by parents into brothels also, in not-
causation in (and) 'flocking' to it — the same halcyon 'flirting' — not
in film (can't record at present, or allow in memory. — only)
                       really 'slight panic as rushing' not-causation
only

                                            (LS)

      The violence there (as I see it — but a whole family is
involved, its "central figure" (as ego?) taking it upon herself)
couldn't be communicated in a string of inquisitive photos: "do I
remember tunneling through limestone?" "do I remember the
German lover or was that the other man on the path?" "do I lie to
tourists?" "will I do (sentimental) 'absolutely anything for them'
(and whose (staked) children are they)?"
      It seems "late" as I write this.
      Do you know what I saw today?
      Canals and hardly wet. I asked: "Whose water is it in those
canals?"
      A dead rat lay at the dry lip of the concrete canal as our
train went past, a man writhing with back pain forced off

      Wanting to come to it
      I'd thought I'd have to get included
      But being physically overeducated or starcrossed (and in the
dark for this reason — secret)
      I got forever caught in the lull
      News

                                              (LH)

      in public casting aspersions to unknown one as if a deeply
horrible person

      the being taught 'intellect' as if it were something — and
emotion, as if something else — isn't — what has always been in
public — ?

      ('their' being — separate — and their being not the same as

well — is hierarchy — and is seeing as it, as 'being' 'being')
this is a violence to public in itself as people flocking to
public in itself — ?
thrown into the dark air — (running with snails)
the ultrasonic cries of the snails, not people
at evening thousands still invading — being only that —

not invisible yet an inversion of their being as if light within
them but as inversion, perceived by outside 'only,' or possibly.
'Wanting to come to it' — one — is the string of such
inverted motions 'only' (as them and as people compressed as action
— not compared), existing only as observed are noticeable in a
created 'outside.'

                                                              (LS)

                          snailing

                    in the separate emotions

                                                              (LH)

        The exchange is tonal imprecations on the invisible — as
impositions on it 'music' — a response.
        Either — one occurs as the other or not — Making a
voluptuous loveliness to be home
        in the child who hasn't been valued also. The invisible
intrinsically a joke.
        The man in the postoffice wouldn't allow a man who'd been
leaving to place my box, which I couldn't lift, on his counter
indicating to place it across the room — the man holding it asking
But how will she carry it?, the postman answering I don't know.
        Maybe he'll be transferred away — ?
        'Going through life' as a stance, emotions — is the
same as if a puritan, emotions — repressed as
impositions — .

        That makes something else from itself? — the imposition of
the holy blind dolphins becoming at present extinct in the Ganges

---

from it.

 We're just sick of it — from it — maybe — the visibility of vomiting in public, as it being it — people vomiting, not viewing one.

(LS)

 Experience ("it is flat") can get dangerously thrown around ("what is the taste of this soup without salt?") in theatrical situations ("I open my mouth; I puke!"). The result is only a semblance of emotion, without emotion's intelligence.

 Emotion's intelligence enables us to 'go through life' (the emotions progress), maneuvering between curses (the question of blessings we'll set aside).

 "How is the weather?"

 "Open your umbrella!"

 Where materiality is concerned, the emotions are crucial to the response:

 "Has Nancy as much money as we two?"

 "No! It is very sad: she has less!"

 But as Saint Augustine points out, though "compassion is commendable it cannot be desirable" since to desire it is to desire the suffering which produces it.

(LH)

 Closing one's umbrella in rain being then emotion's intelligence — as is vomiting, if it is —

 imprecations on the invisible multiplying in paranoia[1] being then a voluptuous rest

 Somehow "compassion" doesn't want the suffering that produced it — that's more piousness, or sentiment (I think). "Compassion" is stronger; is where 'there is no progress'

 [1] one's own

 Liking the image of vomiting clearly.

 It's a sort of Pilgrim's Progress.

 Series of essays as the form being measure

(LS)

A certain genius puts a drunken scorpion on his tongue
The image is that of his open mouth
In the essay the mouth steams but the certain genius can't
say why (i.e., "Why?")
He feels pity, horror, exoticism
He feels progress — as if learning Spanish ("¿con qué
parlamos?")
With what do you feel compassion?

Feeling the trunks of shadows in the image of seeing clearly
I'm at ground level in a redwood forest, conjecturing that I
need the outside world (form is measure in that sense)

(LH)

Maybe vomiting 'clearly' could be connected to compassion?
Scorpion on the open mouth which is vomiting is implied. Even
more, delight. What everyone has and so 'described' as progress
'when seen' but if it's merely clear it's not felt (in one)?[1]

as it's in the charnal hated 'ground' of ego — by being
described — so is described as if not to experience it as *per se* 'not'
ego.
and one being enamoured with drunken
scorpion[2] in itself, which I am immediately when
you say it
[2] "and" — on — one's tongue connected
numbers are here footnotes, objectivity
the bat(ego) in its bow/box (which is hating itself today *per se* being
in it) flies in its charnal 'ground' (hating so it isn't even one? hating
leaps out of oneself?) that's the lighted evening sky above the Taj
Mahal floating jewel — in rushes (isn't even enamoured?)
[1] 'they'

(LS)

We began by leaning, getting out, much as Dorothy
Wordsworth (in delight never for her own sake) must have done,
accumulating sights for her autobiography (autobiography

transposes the character of the teller into the subject of the tale). In
those days (for Dorothy Wordsworth), objects could suffuse one's
subjectivity with their inconsistency.

We transpose them into our own (our ego is set up by our
inconsistency).

We are quick (essayists) walkers, speeding at ground level
(in the garden I like to get up close, as if scuttling onto the visible —
that is, having the perspective of a beetle).

(L commented the other day, "How powerful mythologies
can be! Think of the elevation of the ladybug from the class of
beetles!")

One fine day (cold milky sun on the hoods of cars, rosy
moss crumbling into fissures in the dirt, fern fronds still in the
curled position) some walkers came upon an old dump site and
picked it over, provoking, on the basis of no information at all,
compassion.

(LH)

The turtle (one) cannot even conjure violence lying on its
back — inner and outer violence being the same, and we're in it
anyway, how are we to *get in* it (when we're there) — the turtle
cannot conjure violence in light evening lying (because inner is
incapable and being in outer is in evening there)

it's either no hands, not being a man (if one *is,* even) or
nothing, is too difficult.

Going back — one can't. One is suffering merely
physical nerve lying on ice which is in evening, when in
inner (violence, they want people to be in disturbance
entirely, only) — evening isn't either. Or *in* either.

That eludes one as lying turtle only. Because one is
there. then.

It's either no hands, not being a man in pain (if one *is,* even),
or nothing. No ordering of memories or sights. Dorothy
Wordsworth walks. in outdoor-walks.

People filed differently, in the brain, not thought of
furniture. Objects could suffuse subjectivity with their
inconsistency. Delight itself. Animals' names. Names for

animals as compassion. Blue walking.

What if animals were named that? "An" animal was named that.

What do you suppose *John* thinks of this rest? I know there can be walking.

Out of the blue I ask T "Why don't you ever ask my permission to do things?" Briefly considering he answers, "It never occurred to me." (Peals, rings of laughter from both).

(LS)

The turtle is exemplary in being on its back, midway between flailing (frustrated essaying) and reversing (until the turtle is back up).

Comedy too (provoking laughter) inverts.

And couldn't other reversals (inversions) be such that, when they are successful, as in the case of a collapsed turtle whose limbs (the head and neck comprise a limb) are closed into each other (all of its parts being spatially and temporally simultaneous with each other), we could say, not that "everything is possible," but rather that something else (something and its else) is possible.

Violence has no such manner — no manner (habit, persistence) of being — so it cannot be something else. It cannot be (named) "turtle."

Violence remains in the evening (black) sun. "The turtle," says B, "is reduced to slavery."

B in the dark is comic (comedy always combines). The result might be step coal, puddle pleasant, snow poke ....

"Snow poke?"

Yes!

It is cool and the best part of the day.

The same!

(LH)

Black sun occurring only while walking

The turtle lying on its back — peels flaking — is swimming.
Just think of what one barely accepts what's else being violence.
What one comes up to without being worn out, only pleasurable yet
as just recipient — where other can be without effort. Violence can
too be something else.

Turtle with head and legs sealed within, closed — but only
its being — can't be expressed as an (its) 'impression' on others
occurring. Violence in that sense can move itself. (Having a
manifestation seeming similar)

is violence in relation to image itself? — there swimming
(not related to other association).

slavery isn't expressed as by others. is. lying 'one' is left
behind. enslaving then.

not in evening even.

It reminds me of pithing a frog which we had to do.
never forgotten. can't be reduced to memory.

(LS)

The pithing would be mortifying — and soon afterwards the
child would lose interest in (forget) the (no longer driven by
pleasure) frog

But what if the child 'took chemistry' (imageless black sun)
instead — manifestations without something in the all-girl (gray
skirt) environment — rings of permissive laughter chained (frozen
with fear) over the spot from which the frog left the river —
troubled by (immaterial) symmetry?

Beauty is ideal — ('in the eye') — one seizes one's own
darkness

And one's pleasure causes a certain phrasing — a precise
'zoological' jumping — to the strangest part of being

(LH)

We're neither to worry, or to jump as symmetry — either —
or quiet them
in the strange crevasse, a girl in purdah (normal of her
world) whose brother's friends are so loud partying she hides at the

top of the stairs in her nightgown seeing them and they rape her; her father condemns her, as responsible, to living in a cellar without light for the rest of life, occurring at present. Life resting.

Interfering in the fraternity, is even noting, the live acting — they.

neither blindness or jumping — is called "there." (What's there is not either of those.)

And
man jets on ejaculated stream in field of frogs. As one. As well.

(LS)

The visionary at his stream is off-balance, as if the time for his or her departure (never attaining equilibrium) were drawing near — friends and members of the family are bringing out their cameras, they will complain later that the resulting 'resemblance' is no good

His or her public face is masked by the private one — that which is entirely 'missing'

Meanwhile, a woman all in dark dons her tradition and returns (not driven into hiding without pleasure) to strike angles — posing at the resting wall and then climbing it to picnic at the top

She experiences a reasonable vertigo — a visible experience posited at its vanishing point

weakly into animal
pushed back

(LH)

A long Warhol movie in which we were going to see *Sleep* on a sheet between trees on black night moon

only seeing the other's gestures on the sheet in sleep seen outside

interior annihilated (one's) as superfluous or in exhaustion of days so as to meet (as no resemblance) the woman with head-covering (veiled as ordinary — and/or her in pain, or not)

not faceless but as in *Sleep* the movie being at night — only.
Her translated in some 'place' where she is not as one's
viewing is superfluous even. Or not because *it* is.

(LS)

In sleep in the camps hand folding was forbidden — hands
lay open, left out (the interior omitted) — exteriority was in force
This altered the context phrase: *in sleep*

Some shouting is occurring out of sight — it is a raucous
extension of a man's voice with wheedling but arrogant overtones
supplicating or summoning someone or something called "Baby" or
demanding that this someone or something do it: i.e., "Baby"
The shouting man is experiencing a failure of independence

(LH)

I was experiencing a failure of independence by sleeping —
as sleeping, yet needed, worn out — involuntary superfluity. Of
night, as huge clouds are in it.
The sleep was in day, however. In day I see fields of erect
orange lilies, tiger lilies.
I read that 'minorities' are now not being given jobs in labor
as there are fewer jobs for the majority race. Foremen call the
people they know, acknowledging they would not want to be the
other race.
Intellect isn't an entity, but solely a relation to — action.
Failure of independence in shouting is outcome of memory
going back to — (finally) unrelated

To relate as 'tell' something as action only. Unconsidered.
In the first dream life was void, and in the second one it was
too — I was writing them down for you while in them. I was in the
middle of the two, the second having occurred in the future. In the
second, something about spitting in a large donkey's eye. ('Good
sense').

(LS)

The donkey (like Balaam's ass) is a seer (of angels, according to legend, and of women's secrets). That's why sometimes the gossiping Sibyl (and sometimes the tale-telling Mother Goose) is shown in old pictures (lifting her skirt out of the dust on a road or hitching it up to ford a stream) with one human foot and one donkey hoof.

When the donkey speaks it tells what it sees — is the tale really without consideration?

I suppose so. So then when women spit in a donkey's eye it's to make it cry (not to blind it).

When Ralph Waldo Emerson was first coming into his own (around 1828) as a thinker he made what he called a "frank acknowledgement of unbounded dependence" —

as if at an horizon (in that middle) —

between (dreams) dramas —

having (like us) dramas *for someone else*

Here I'm (looking back over these past few lines) thinking that a definition of (psychological) drama might posit it as a 'telling' which is rendered into 'action only' — but I'm not, like you, a playwright, and I'm not sure that this is the good sense of it.

But I can see that drama renders Mother Goose's dreams independent.

(LH)

Black bombing wasps — one is a censor swaying to one up the flight of stairs.

On a stream with one human foot and one donkey foot.

Sand, heat, rubble where they made only obstinate destructive moves already. You can't have a wallet. Without one you can't walk. One can't speak. Feels a sense of tears.

I don't know why it was unconsidered. It occurs, is considered later, and consideration isn't the source.

Moon isn't the source of ground on which flies land of course.

One's dress dragging is covered with piss in the stream. Outside one. Events. Not seeing the different things at once — is a different seeing — which there is being in the middle in the

continuum double dream as well. One isn't in the later dream yet
and has had it writing it in it.

(LS)

An older person in events is aided by a younger one who
presses against her from behind to "further" the (languid scenario)
continuity
    The face of one of them is bitten
    The resulting crescent-shaped scar is like ...
    But at this point in the narrative the one questions: "Do you
remember how much of a nuisance you were?" "Donkey loose in
the vineyard?"
    The considerate one asks — "Covered over by water
swaying?"
    The rhetoric of questions repeats: rising tone, rising tone,
etc. "Who or what was swaying?"
    The day (flying land) was hot. Or I'm confusing description
with invention, compassion.
    Does compassion play on coincidence confusing continuity?
    That isn't a rhetorical question; (continuity is inside).

    I smelled the asparagus in the piss — not an invention: green
and dragging (etched) in the stream. I wondered if I should reassure
(the foreigner newly perhaps pissing this odor) him. Then the event
broke off.

(LH)

    Or confusing embarrassment with the seeing of imageless
black sun. Crouching in the blackness which is also shining and
crackling — one is in the landscape in its only occurrence.
    So continuity is subject to sight only
    Amongst them crouching is the face of one, bitten — a scar
on it like a pond, the bitten face is held under water — There's only
continuity in two.
    Someone being in their hospital room, at dawn — had the
same sense of intense pleasure — *as being* dawn, after it — The
location occurs by virtue of its dawn. The sun not coming up, there.

Embarrassment as continuous clarity
Another memory (of pithing a frog, which brought up great
guilt) rather than dimming occurs while crouching in the crackling
black light. I have too many continuities. The light has the same
weight as eating hurriedly. *Yet drinking dark blood red wine in the
black light without weight*
        The intense pleasure of watering is in light evening then

                                                                    (LS)

        With a little quiver, the lookout in her car casting about for
a memory, parked near a cyclone fence in an industrial district
severed from a freeway by a dark crescent-shaped pond
        The commission of a crime occurring abruptly
        And for an instant without room
        Which the next instant the crime requires
        For dying act and observer

        Or a good thing
        One of those which we don't just accept but choose
        By signing on to understand and to make understood
        We're advocates
        In small visible attempts at being pleasing
        Or invisible in the lookout's (which can't be imageless)
memory

                                                                    (LH)

        A dark bank by a crescent-shaped pond of blood — the
moon doesn't emerge from it. Not causal therefore.
        It is also a bank with tellers in it, in slots their eyes sewn
shut.
        (The bank is by the bank — one of the tellers has red lips, a
man, but his eyes sewn shut have still images, vertical — with no
base, not in repetition either).
        I came to the conclusion that I can't relate motions to myself
(as those being me), just as my mother and later myself (to) hurl
oneself without contemplation, at a bicycle to mount it for example
— neither there when riding in a black sunlit afternoon.

Without contemplation has images. Crimes being committed, the dead people aren't huge brown and indigo butterflies.

But they are those butterflies as sight. Our friend's mother and sister kidnapped, the mother beheaded after being tortured, the sister tortured her ear cut off, our consulate won't allow her to come to this country to rest not a butterfly.

(LS)

I want to say something, then, about the impossibility of testing the "atrocity" in the blank at the person's eyes

Something can be true there even if in negation, as a lie

That is, it may be true that something horrible (beyond testing) has occurred but it comes to a stop, in disfigurement without transformation — fluttering

Though a description has been made of it in timeless terror, if we hold that description of it to the mirror, no image of it will appear there

The atrocity is the blank — a blank transition

Our thoughts are deprived by atrocity of objects to move between

Transit is blocked

I understand this from reading Jalal Toufic's *(Vampires):* she is undead

standing, in legal despair, denuded by questions, barred, dishevelled by a long shiver, with her sentiments relegated to an incomprehensible church, her coat inside out (as if turned against her)

(LH)

Losing short-term memory utterly, of even a moment before — by being exhausted cumulatively, suddenly she passed into only remembering years before and who we were, she had "forty-eight hour amnesia" in order to rest — predictably she revived: experience tested in being lost — in forty-eight hours she returned to the present

I would like to "go somewhere" there, as in seeing the dye

filling which was a pond inside my left side not seen on my eyes

This could be the undead? — though they roiling on the (dead as blank) blue night have to bite into the necks of people in the present incomprehensibly. Atrocity (to the crowds bitten) being just when *they* wake.

They have being only in relation to people — is that it? Some people lie yelling not remembering, having had strokes.

Yet the blank transition and some other experience in it is without flowers, court life at the capital? ... or is slowly only the present.

Extreme experience in a blank 'transition,' the blank could become the place for some other experience?

— not addicted to living

(LS)

A woman without short-term memory can only begin to be a woman without short-term memory. Then she is gone — *per se.* So it is only at the beginning that she screams. Why did I scream?

from what I select ... flirting who? and zeroing ... at the bruised finger ... time has ... a clown gem ... in vast rolling chest sex ... my proof attracted into the neck ... hurling to an unforgettable evening ... when ... I select

(LH)

I dreamt, when I was in fact traveling, that I met Carla — but having nothing to do with "traveling," happening to — and the sole thought nothing said, as a revelation and alleviating, "there's no reason (that people can) not to enjoy people / that it's possible / enjoyment of people."

Content is "akin to" dream of meeting you and, before but at the same time of the occurrence having the thought "that all of life is void" which I knew you'd want to hear rushing up to you, you were smiling, nothing said — the now earlier thought in it "having to do with *now* spitting in a donkey's eye." It didn't have to do with (or did?) words — perhaps single ones. Before them. But

83

occurs in words after. Spitting in a donkey's eye doesn't occur, and isn't in words (while it's in the dream), isn't aggressive.

(LS)

Awake I hear (in the voice of Jalal Toufic), "Time is the element that permits invisibility."

Time *is* invisible, that's clear, but it is because of time that juxtaposition, friendship, love, measure, etc. can be (invisible), so.

All reserve disappears. No one will know.

Z calls from Holland. "Music," he says, "kills time through accentuation."

Unwinding the psychological film the breaks in astonishing life flicker. A woman's chest heaves, empties. It is an unusually warm October and the transition between moments is becoming difficult.

In the true (incorrigible) cheerfulness of dream (under pressure) anything that is broken might represent open arms, spread legs — as in the spread legs of the donkey-rider between whose arms the soft animal neck bobs. Away from this scene, I become a woman being "intellectual" among men whom no women will join intellectually.

Whatever is meant by kindness becomes confused — is apple "akin to" a donkey's ass?

(LH)

I was noticing that spitting in the donkey's eye hadn't occurred as an action in the dream — but occurs 'in some time' in the dream, in the 'past' yet 'when' the image first comes up (at the instant it comes up in it — yet not as an action 'then' at the time of coming up)?

So any event is awakened/killed — as being is its own time? — doesn't occur ever but seems to have happened. One doesn't have to be afraid to do it and it is necessary.

One is nothing in the sense of merely observed, a contralto singing. Riding a donkey between one's legs.

The neck bobs as oneself gently has walked also, legs spread on it.

Yes, donkey's ass is an apple, when seen. At that moment 'akin to' crowds, in revolution.

Plazas of water in which crowds thrash, falling down, attempting to seize apples with their teeth.

(Are not invisible places but reappear exactly, the crowds sliding struggling for the apples. Intellect is merely will, [its content is not different from having legs spread; there is nothing to join] — seen as 'before death' only, either cheerful or churlish ...)

(LS)

Perhaps we can only enter (at the point where there is *nothing-to-join*) at infinite speed (at anything less we'll be left for dead) through banality: "I'm going to check into a motel."

In the scenario I'm out of dream.

I start to discuss a collection (as condescension) — it is arranged into a display of figurines cast during the 1850s (the years that saw the publication of Marx's *Capital*, Darwin's *Origin of the Species*, Flaubert's *Madame Bovary* and Ruskin's *Modern Painters*, when "America," to quote Theodore Dreiser,"was just entering upon a most lurid phase").

The display is entirely static (being a collection) — but I find myself out of dream anxious.

I'm thrashing.

A great cow is led through the kitchen with its tail up.

I'm slow.

Perhaps we can only enter as children do — unprepared but in play.

If I say, I'll be the lion tamer and you be the radio announcer and then together we put the pair of lovebirds in their cage on a kitchen stool at which I crack a whip and you say, "Folks, this is incredible," that's play.

If I say I'll do something, I'll do it — that's performative.

I'm saying what I mean, with the orbit of what I'll do (in

circus) visible (to be viewed).

(LH)

I was coming out of a gathering with the leaving crowd and
heard someone remarking with inclusive interest, as if at one (with
each other), that so-and-so was walking, with someone — "that's
her father." Mine came towards us.

He said to the passing younger throng — him being jovial as
information which also expresses a view (as if giving a talk), that the
bureaucrats or officials who met here (at this park we were
entering) — tended — (as if) in that era (including — earlier) — to go
to jail. (To end in jail — as if corrupt [or revolutionaries] regardless
of the park, a meeting place) we went to the cliff, the park being:
where the elephants suckle their young — peering over, I saw in the
ocean water elephants on their sides floating swaying as if in dance
equidistant curled (hundreds) suckling — "But where are the
young?" — who must have been under the water invisible — the
trunks of the elephants trays were honeycombed grey trays

in the latter part — is neither anxious or separated from the
dream
the divinity of another poet which is excluding everyone —
and destroying her young (to be viewed by her:) *consciously* to do
so. — *later,* after the dream occurred. But I am not a poet — (even)
— (not even that) — separated and out of the dream.

(LS)

What enormous resistance the certain have to a reality
which is entirely thought — a ponderous ("manned") resistance,
when the reality requires speed.

Such speed would not be the (possessive) speed "of an
animal" but speed *as* an animal.

Thought always exists in the realm of "*as* reality" — all that
is thought manifests an "as effect."

We have no case for it, but it is instrumental.

"I ran fast as a horse."

If one were (briefly) to become a horse "regardless of the park," one could do so with certitude, not in action (that is, not through superfluous meditation) and not in the moment (for example, in water), but at the point of "a prison break" — (as (in) difference) so that one would no longer be comparable *per se* to a prisoner, having run fast, say, as a horse, and therefore one could see that one was (literally and freely between the incommensurate planes of prisoners and horses) an incorrigible.

(LH)

I ran as a horse. We have utter madness — (and) a place and condition in it that C would say is funny.

I always think I have to be someone else literally, to force this one to change, without knowing who oneself is, knowing one's habits.

The halves of the person squatting from running urinating

That's one action. When one is a horse — one's two halves have *two* legs running.

Of course one could run at the exact pace of a certain horse during a prison break. Authority can't be evanescence

Yet this is different from what people say is "self-expression."

Which is their madness. One experiences one's own fastness thus. in theirs.

Yet thus — one's — fastness — occurs there simply

(is it that it is better to be a horse? — in a play or music is fictional time as one's time.)

So a place and condition in it has *its* 'real time,' which is only *its* own sense of time, has a measure and space, what's occurring in it may not even be seen. But occurs there as having times — Beside/by the viewers.

(LS)

I find myself listening to music as if struggling against inevitability — it and I are *(as)* one, at the limit, and I'm about to make one of those ludicrous false steps that fell one. That's fate: I can't go on (with remorse and regret). Like the philosopher I must say, I'm no one's guilty conscience, and certainly not my own

— rain freezing on slick asphalt, people falling, perhaps I'm feverish, I want to see — I seem to be the only one who isn't cold — but then a suicidal riderless horse dragging its reins appears, eyes wide, neck broken, head bent to the right, chest straining, it moves against orders — every struggle for thought pits the ponderous against the fast — yes, well, so as to hide but also so as to see, they eat into each other's lips, that's what it's like to say inevitability can't be unemployed —

in a struggle.

The successful struggler must constantly add positions. She jumps graciously out of the field with her skirt up and into an interval. This event has its own duration — it doesn't "unfold over time," it remains in its fold, employed —

her great neck wet with sweat from pulling.

(LH)

The suicidal riderless horse wide-eyed, neck broken already, is the emanation of one to oneself in exhaustion [in the case of your having cancer] but appearing to others "inevitably" — who are unemployed in the sense of happening by chance to be seen there also, not 'for a purpose.'

The struggler in the state of exhaustion is the observer within that one — "within" is what unfolds though not appearing to, not caused by exhaustion, separately transpiring to a clear aim (not in apprehension).

The viscous wet neck after it is dawn — one having missed seeing dawn/separation — has its own duration, apart from that observer

the eyes are not of the neck
wide-eyed the neck being a 'mere' appendage
flapping

(LS)

The neck of a sibling being is visible in the shadow (the rider feels the weariness of false choices)

Faltering
     — visibility *makes* the being
        lean over
    "marking out form"

Coupled to visibility's trembling form
Eyed by inevitability

But, really, inevitability is what accumulates ahead of false continuities

(LH)

Visibility makes what is seen — ? — Empty careening head that is in angry circular rushes, where there isn't substance for these it occurs anyway — as its physiological habit.
       ghosts are only during someone's life.
    So they're making the life going on past occurrence. Which could be then pleasurable.
    The wild motions in one are seen and their former substance or origination is a 'visibility' itself — which may be hardly remembered or remembered with utter clarity — but the tortured wild motions in one would occur anyway.
    Without what bothers one. (Yet one is tortured.)
    The Romantics either European or Japanese were perhaps the discoverers that one is living-ghosts as being present activity — not being of dying — dying seems utterly separate.
      fear is expanded —

(LS)

A ghost comes "to work on the wall" — very expressive activity for the living previous person, the one existing before it cast its ghost, but the ghost is, as it were, working on the wrong side (the outside — *beyond the limit*) of the wall.
    Working loudly, but this work is a past occurrence —

carried out by someone very beautiful (in "wild motions") — the
ghost doesn't offer a smile of recognition.

Jalal Toufic says the great problem for the dead is that of
continuation (unfinished business). (The ghost) it has the problem
of not being there where it hasn't been — a problem of regret, yes,
but also of self-replication: (the ghost) any self is constantly
remaking the person from which it was cast to no end.
The sudden (shown up) death of a youth (unfinished) is
separated from him by a narrator.

(LH)

We're on the level here of winter light only — no one out —
yet in it trees enflamed in a red leaves sea.
the one dead isn't fatigued

Whereas work in jobs for living — generates more and more
of itself only. — There is a sole consciousness existing in winter
light, so that is apart from one too.
The sole consciousness (of ones) that begins to exist in red
leaves sea aflame only — outside — isn't part of a dead person or
one
self-replication — a double which is also sole, empty
fear that in living ones working on the wrong side of
the wall with those others (dead) being on that side, the same side of
the wall — and can't be to be there
a double membrane — who may be one — though can't be
with them
people clamor as in a bureaucracy — for more and more
events — the one without a soul isn't drunk. — In loneliness and
beached — the wild motions do not meet up
yet — Occur — as them — attentiveness to oneself, who is
not existing

(LS)

A person suffering, a person at a distant place, the very
place he or she may be, a person close to dying — turning inward —
out of the body cavity oneself — turns to the interior of a thought

90

(wall)

> — at the thought
>   cavity, phrasing
> long before photography
>   — that just preserves food
>
>   laziness means being slower
>   than oneself
>   — and unsexed in absence
>   of stretched, distracted parts

But to return, we were saying, "between," even to very fast music and a flash alligator rolling between gallant lilies. Then a couple from Minnesota appears in a red and gray camper and wearing *only* binoculars. They are elderly — in the motel, turning on the light — a distracted part larger than the universe unrolled — in the camper with a bird book. The woman is very kindly and points out (action? non-action?) an ibis — the universe — in focus.

(LH)

(just preserving food — in one) — osmosis is not reflected, anywhere
    outside the lily fields by the roads(:) are then not inverting
— are slower than oneself, outside phenomena then exist.
    osmosis (which is reflection) — isn't reflected (itself)

    but phenomena are only that when
    the blind (dilated) in oneself, (as while asleep actions are
'contentless' — *is* seeing?)
    "Mass sociogenic illness" is reported as the cause of acute outbreaks of unexplained illness in school settings. Characteristics of such outbreaks are lack of illness in others sharing the same setting, headache, nausea, weakness, hyperventilation, fainting, a preponderance of cases among females, and "line-of-sight" transmission.
    It is transmitted by "line-of-sight" — contentless in that one sees someone and one's condition is transmitted to them. (also ceases reflection?)
    not fabrication but detection

(LS)

One constantly produces didactic situations.

In poetry?

I give a description of a perception — a particular perception, concerning the activity of the description itself of regarding an object of experience, in which language renders a particular 'reality' uncertain even though logic keeps checking and repeatedly ascertains that it (whatever it is) is really there — and this is taken as "doubtful."

So Ponge is right when he says, "We must choose true objects, constantly objecting to our own desires. Objects that we would select again and again, and not as our decor or milieu; rather like our spectators, our judges; without our being, of course, either dancers or clowns."[1]

By the way, it's true that someone's adoring gaze has, in the past, filled me with adoration.

Then what? Accuse him or her of being too didactic?

Dream that the will is only at work in waking life? or that lilies by the roads only "dance" in the wind when we see them?

[1] In "The Object is Poetics"

(LH)

Line-of-sight vomiting struck me as very delightful.

One's adoring of someone occurring outside of (underlying) waking life — has overflowed 'gaze.' As their (in people) vomiting is no longer inner — any logic being a mere 'object' (an objective) itself, impermanent.

The people vomiting at once by line-of-sight transmission — occurs only with people, yet is the inner 'being' in the outer.

It (anything) may be didactic and without one ever knowing what one is learning.

The will being at work in waking life, yet waking life itself occurs while asleep, invading itself — from reverse, rather than the dreaming entering any waking activity (during a period then).

Another time, a dream will impinge and burst in on a waking activity at a moment, so both are rendering uncertain states as activity *per se.*

(LS)

Waking life gets distributed as narrative through footnotes and applied to dreams when dreams are divided from waking life. What in dream were 'paradoxical faces' get interpreted as expressive personifications and are presumed to be masks out of which the dreamer is vomiting. For the dreamer to be vomiting *in a way that makes sense,* the mask must be removed. The school (didactic) setting prompts (after separation) empty vomiting — into the gap between waking and dream, one might say, or between 'this time' and 'another time.'

Every day of the week except Fridays I get up at 6:45 a.m. but on Thursdays by 5:45 a.m. I've already been awake for 4 hours during which I've been experiencing (in sight, as waking dreams) pure effects (causeless) — colors without what they color, persons independent of faces. Sometimes, just as I think I'm about to fall asleep I say to myself that I've got to get some sleep. That is marked language. The language of waking life is always marked. In order to have real dreams, one has to sacrifice those marks — but this isn't to say that dreams don't love logic. The capacity to see in dreams is logical — a morality in progress?

(LH)

There's a lid on waking life in someone undercutting faces — rather than the faces being independent in waking life — only
— then a dream is divided from waking life precisely by being in it? — it being independent

dismiss (didactic) the vomiting dreamer (as one) — the act (of vomiting) being being in waking life even asleep dreaming it. No physical act existing of it in waking, how can one be waking? — drives backward vomiting: I've always liked that as a gap which is urgent yet circular and an outside motion, a motion outside of one.
A dream being marked also, as 'coming from' waking life *so that* a scrap of it recognized later in waking life has no marking.

(LS)

Waking life is disordered by chance (yet circular and in

outside motion: waking life, disorder, and chance).

It is chance that forms the continuous present moment (which is always completely separate from the past and future) — as (in gap) becoming: the one incessant chance

> with a setting element: the prolongation
> into (these, those — deixis
> in other words) marks of everything
> in sight

There's someone who might be a busy person, seated, and also an alligator's head severed just behind the eyes, streaks of rain, clay pots draped with ferns on a balcony enclosed in wrought iron vines, a sudden sound eliciting brief vision (warehouse in flames). One is required to fill out a questionnaire in order *to pass inspection* — does one fly frequently into rages? does one rampage? does one consider (or has one ever considered) suicide? does one feel that others are 'always' (or frequently) 'in the way'? is one startled by sudden loud noises in the dead of night?

I saw the trick — the affirmation (*'yes!'*) that was supposed to appear — as the mark of having really taken the test — having surrendered to inspection. Has one been injured? does one suffer from frequent stomach problems? is one vomiting?

(LH)

> passing inspection — which is also the coughing — night's doing so — the boards slap on bellies as they strike the river — to sense of aberration

Seeing people as 'their' — the banks (where money is kept also) not even in moonlight being yet the boards that are crocodiles hitting the river at once (thousands hurling from the bank) as 'one' on a balcony — so no structure exists in night — surfing — where having entered the water the thousands of crocodiles slap as boards in moonlight (is 'first' 'at' night?) — to go after a 'one' 'there' is 'disorder'?

> *theirs* is — in the moonlight?

(LS)

94

One passes through inspection asking questions: what do you hear? what do you see? Sudden loud noises continue to elicit images: a bolt of lightning elicits an egret. *Yes!*

One takes on inspection by asking questions, counting to zero, drawing toward a rim of vulnerability (an incessant singularity) at the edge of sight.

(LH)

yes. sleeping in happiness — aberrations
sloughs — as seeing? ('first') moonlight) [not at the same time]

peering on dams — crowds as we pass through on a ship lightning [not at the same time] no disorder occurs, one's rim
isn't in one — (both large and small is rim)
they —
are (as 'violating' pair — as peering on dams) — one doesn't overwhelm

(LS)

One is cold in the water and sleeping in happiness and one can experience these as inexhaustible from reflection in a ripple (in repetition) because they are *not at the same time.* Where it's *all at the same time* is an awful limbo.
The inhabitants are afraid of what they might see. They fear loss without loss occurring.

T says we've aestheticized when we're happy with some rusty wreck in the landscape, but I (fighting the negative implications of aestheticization) argue that what we've done is to evaluate the wreck. T, however, is right. We've released the wreck, it's independent of us. No one left it there to spoil our view.
The aesthetic is that which is not at the same time.
It's what Agnes Martin calls 'wild brushstroking.' The interviewer (Joan Simon [in *Art in America,* May 1996, page 84])

95

asks her, "What was it about this line that has kept you sustained for 30-odd years," and she answers, "It looks good to me."

(LH)

To be awed — as to walk as a visitor — in Dante's hell — only — and happiness one's being only a visitor [*at the same time* — as Dante's hell] there
an awful limbo in water with no lines
wrecks (of cars) in all the fields, the trees destroyed by foresters
I dreamed of a friend agreeing to lunch with my grandmother who's dead, my attempting to unite the two by my being in a car narrowing the distance though they were both in the same realm at either end — and I was not — I usually recognize her as being dead, her face averted not speaking to me, but didn't — averting his face he doesn't come to lunch. I then thought he'd died. I hadn't spoken to him in nine years. He called me to say "I had a dream about you. We were to go to lunch but then we were not going — " is — Agnes Martin's 'extreme' happiness as 'extreme' only. There.

(LS)

Comedy (it's imminent — a point of view that convinces us that this is beautiful provides comic potential) narrows a distance without ever reducing it.
A naked sweet dream figure standing in pink and misty dappled sunlight under branches heavy with peaches says, Watch out, if it's narrow it's deep.
Such warnings (they assume that visible things are omens) are aphoristic.
I take an auspicious stick and look out into the orchard.

You can't just record beauty, Agnes Martin says. Of course not, you can't even just see it. Beauty isn't just it.
There's the white line, too, and missing lunch.
Is that which is far inside the narrow 'extreme'? Is that what you mean?

(LH)

I was thinking of 'extreme' — as "I can think what I like"
(your words) — freedom, *only*
('extreme') as if defined by others (yet why so? — I imposed
the narrow view) — and if so ("defined"), then, not existing as
freedom — 'extreme' is existing only. No one needs to worry.
Thinking [my] the man had died was inaccurate — as the
dream. It was my grandmother wasn't (dead)

"she is in 'the realm of death' when she died — but isn't now"
(dreamed words)
which isn't the same as being in hell as a visitor —
which is only living
— "I can think what I like" — : my mind is the phenomena —
then — Agnes Martin's 'extreme' (my word) happiness is expansive
— as being-unknown

(LS)

One is happy in one's susceptibility to chance, accident,
hazard
So a descriptive sentence (being an account of what unfolds
to sensibility) may be precarious and must be careful
As something's happening
The sentence says so with felicity — that's what one might
get when writing in sight with happy exactitude
In the realm of death, too
Each thing, no matter how happy in its word, is ('only')
floated
In the realm of life, too

A hummingbird in the morning flies right up to me at the
door and stays in the air

(LH)

— even if she wasn't [past] where at dawn on gorges burning
the tar — migratory labor on roads — as it being at dawn 'only' there

'accident' of birds [that are] being in space. — singing too

97

only floating in the realm of life too — are they at [their]
present and past (at the same time) — and separately
    which is the space [them]
    — the figures the same as space, no other phenomena —
'something's happening' is this too
    these blossoms purple-white-fringed blooming in the time
away from them — and before — at the same time as 'one' is happy

                                                        (LS)

    The hummingbird is busy with the mass of sensations, 'up'
and 'down,' advancing and receding, among cascades of accidental
purple morning glories hanging (where they weren't meant to be)
from a tree
    Still the air sustains the sensation of relevance — that this is
'meant to be' — but the hummingbird flying about in it seems to go
to one side
    Then the tree acts as an 'anchoring point' so the garden has
'top' and 'bottom'
    The hummingbird makes a 'correction' — backs

    "I" am still, so this is a still — in motion, blooming, and
fringed, in continuation
    While this vocabulary, which is still, for seeing — another at
the same time — we pass

                                                        (LH)

    blue children walked by the railroad track too
    there aren't any 'accidents' — of motor boats — on the indigo
air — and in space throughout — land patches
    [motorboats are a compound mind's ear, not beginning in
the ear but in the trees
    people are the same as them as children solely

    — ? —] [returning only to their feet on the cake of ice] —
nothing in sleep is necessary but *sleep* is (th*INK* of the Saudis) —
still the air sustains the sensation of 'ones' (only) sleep — to one
people swaying

                                                        98

motorboats blossom opening on the trees —
neither waking — or: with the hummingbird on the ice
field

(LS)

Flying out with a sword and (in one leap) sighting and
raising a prospect: this act
            inducing myriad recurrences
            of *it,* the switchover

It takes the ice, a tiny compound, from half an inch away, as
if terrified of it, ground into a fluttering red hole
            rising backward

                a man (friend)
                        in a banana yellow wig —
                        a switchover
                one sees all but the recurrence

                the man (friend throughout,
                        in folds) is leaning
                        from the feet: to switch
                to the cold wig

(LH)

A cold wig — ice cap —
terror of being plugged into [only] oneself. —
impermanently, physically

            which is not only one / black sky with no stars
            skating (or fighting — yet solely) on the road in night
walking there. external in the sense of no hole coming from one —
happy
            fluttering red hole in sky is in day
            A geographical space that's images (photos) in

which are extended locations made at intersections in rooms with the outside, individuals and their (outsider culture) images (such as pictures on the wall in the photo) beside them — that therefore exists on its own in the actual wide 'geographical / and conceptual space' alien to it.

(LS)

       Waking after night (extending patience) involves more than opening one's eyes upon intersections

                                 on the color-
beginnings of flatness

                drawn out
It takes space to render as an abstraction the positive existence of time

             with the act of identifying the scene
postponed

         until 'the vanishing days'

      In the cold, water blowing

                     its identity
                     an aftermath

                            revolving
                 from the continuous range
           floated
Waking from an inch away

                    to see the object-
beginnings of the outside
        — bald image

(LH)

     the positive image as flatness the same as 'the vanishing days' — where one'd seen the isolated negative image — as object existing

     there is a free-floating ease forward that is — evening rain-lakes — isn't one — though the rain-lakes rising on the fields isn't that ease — is 'from' that ease — ? 'from' 'one' [at the same time] —

rain-lakes 'are' — [first]

(LS)

    A 'nocturnal' ease is one in which one is awake late and not
held back
                  as one is when walking with less vigorous girls
until infinitely alone
                seized by sand

    Giving way underfoot the unsteadiness continues and the
ground still seems to flee
                  still softer because trampled by others
    Ease
        where insects' footprints could be seen

(LH)

is   seized by sand
      night 'is'   sand of desert
'woman seated at tea' outside afternoon   without mark

black roses/not ones   only ease is nocturnal for me in having to see
the day as

        being 'at' night — to see it — still and softer as a result
the day   by   in   blackness
      polar   real   the weaker girls

(LS)

    All the lives of all the girls who attended the grammar
school within *now* (softened) landscaped play areas taken together
'at' night subside amid obscurities and glimmers
                        of the common
dream (of appearing in pajamas) of an intimate 'shared' history of
having to see the day
        in its small milks

The girls causing their dresses to spread out by twirling and
then allowing them to return to hide their thighs in the cold
question: narrative and/or science?
                                        are they in the middle
or on the border?

                                                            (LH)

        contemplative life that is world instigated by

— plagued by borders — girls, being young having nights which is
huge (the small experience that is night fitted into theirs) — and
alone 'woman seated at tea' with vast brilliant shining dress not even
light playing in it which is rich/itself a middle(?) as if thighs shone
through it within and being the landscape — that isn't the future of
the girls
                they have sensation of never having worried

                                                            (LS)

        Lovers ('at the pole of doubt') lie — interwining legs — at
night
        In the bright daylight (on thighs) the girls in their anonymity
adhere to being
                        bright
        A mouse scampers across the threshold where the moon
shines

        They jump in the light playing over ropes
                                                'differing
things'

        Something bad may chance or this
                                        in the future,
an overcoming
                        or good luck
        At day's and night's propinquity
        The girls' eyes closed inside

                                                            (LH)

                                _____

Flying oneself (yet so much earlier it isn't one) as if with no muscles on rings on ropes crossing sawdust so there is no 'depth' of memory and with no muscles flying — one's eyelids open but 'not having to do with' seeing though a sight-memory of moving on the rings through 'no' buoying (isn't memory) rather is weight here, at bottom — there isn't future

I keep forgetting — something coming up (anything) — 'something bad may happen' but that itself is 'sensation of never having worried' then or as adult.
        the child and ring's nothing as luck — yet no future

                                                (LS)

Still, one doesn't let oneself go completely freehand
        one's not at sea in this flying open stroke by stroke
        where one leaves off another begins seeing it first
        it's visible just outside
        hardly worrisome

This luck as time cycles ...
        there we are
        anecdotes everywhere

                                                (LH)

Here — being happy — meaning having been of the elect — and who are therefore prosperous in present, (Calvinism) — suffering is not having been a good person (when?) [blind cycles — beforehand] — people in the ditch suffering were (are) interiorly inferior
        persons inferior indicated by the indication they're suffering — cycles of day and night galvanizing
        seen one as a person suffering swims in ditches of manure — the legs moving thickly are the obverse of illumination — as freehand here
        let go completely freehand
        in isolation of location *per se*, which is neither romantic nor damned — anywhere

question whether so-and-so is liked or so-and-so is liked
    seen the manure beds tunneling by tall sky-glazed grain bins
(not memory — or only an element is — and that existed in other
people
    beggars pushing on cart of hand-held children as relation to
other (utter) [hearing] location — and freehand to one too

(LS)

I would grimace were the cart to teeter, after a change of
subject smiling in vivacious indication, mirroring, then, *this,* the
reflector, not glass but face, 'the obverse of illumination,' changing
the relation, one not of similitude and not a causal one, the change
of face expressing a relation developed (over time) in the face of art
— technique, craft (which 'existed (exists) in other people'), the
manifestation of one's capable knowledge in the ways of making,
being, or doing something.

When a circumstance doesn't exist in other people the
expression *to* it can't exist, but as Wordsworth's rural type pulls his
cart into the world, the children call happily, Look! eager to point
out.

(LH)

Not beholden to their confinement
    the ways of making, being, and doing something — *are* in
the crowds surrounding carts — children pulling — by sky-glazed
grain bins, and there's a change in the sky light
    reflectors are a wind — that's the physical suction the same
(in the same spot) as the children pulling — the wind isn't simply
with them, it *is* the children there
    is a feeling of one (then, later? — it occurs to one — when
not a child) being happy — the expression of it exists neither in the
daylight or weighing with the flowering fields during the night —
obverse illumination (wind) in night while the children calling are in
day there (then and at their / one's present)

(LS)

Then what one might call *an occasioning* (haphazardness) may be the entire content of happiness, precisely, though it's often rendered sloppily, occurring at the moment when one sees *there's a chance*, "a feeling of one" (with the contrivance (sky-glaze) of daylight merely to increase the strength and the definition of the shadows (which we ordinarily don't attend to, except as they help us to perceive the objects of which they are the shade) on the world they shadow)

In Wordsworth (e.g., *The Prelude*), such layering of sensory experience makes *time* and *subjectivity* one (or equal in the eyes of literature) (built on degrees of adventure)

But life now is bordered in a new way (since time is staging one of its periodic uprisings (haiku[1] shows how little is needed to simulate a world))

[1] See Alan Liu, "Local Transcendence: Cultural Criticism, Postmodernism, and the Romanticism of Detail" in *Representations* 32, Fall 1990

(LH)

Perceiving only on shadow is the place where things meet that have no occurrence together or comparison to each other? — no relation, yet there's a new occurrence in 'between' them
    as subjectivity *not* in one, as the sky is in one.
    such as just clear sleep. yet if there're dreams one doesn't even meet them, not fit one to it in it at all. Or several of them *is* in days? [as you are having the radiation after chemo]

    occurrences are only uprisings — and there are other that aren't there?
    memory of summer before one — though there's one — and nights, nothing in between them.

(LS)

One ("I") finds a creek, clear water descending — man with his head in a bucket — over rocks which elevate the clear water, floating one's face
    But the light is inadequate, there's no face, or the light is

'superb, on shadow' without blur of reflection, one can see to the bottom — jaw drops, man calls

The man calls into water
Conventionally, they say that 'the man' is the subject and 'calls into water' is the predicate. But how are we certain that the subjectivity here called 'the man' isn't in fact precisely 'called into water'?
One wades, the creek rolling, splashing over objects difficult to see — man with rocks on his toes

(LH)

The subjectivity *is* 'called into water' as being the man — as 'speaks into her ear' [she is still there] at dying
It seemed so difficult to die — we spoke to her — and she heard
The clear water elevating his face so that the man calls into water being behind in it
There cats on fences as oneself in bucket.

Or hopping in the night with one's feet in a burlap bag on a field in flares, fireworks there — on a lit blackness occasionally.
In night as day there is no moment without a cat in it at this place — one place.

(LS)

One names herself into the ear of a listener, inviting the listener to see with the named one's eyes.
The listener is a negative *per se*, an audience awaiting that sight *at one place*
coming to light
in name only a
foreshadowing.

One goes backward in time (the negative of name) at the sound of the name to something she remembers
as if every

sound were the assertion of something potentially (eventually *to be*)
visible, even if only a movie (mutation)

$\qquad\qquad\qquad\qquad\qquad$ (or play) of life

$\qquad$ (abstracted)

$\qquad\qquad\qquad$ from performance

$\qquad\qquad\qquad\qquad\qquad\qquad$ on logs in

dappled light, mute.

$\qquad\qquad\qquad\qquad\qquad\qquad\qquad\qquad\qquad$ *(LH)*

night is mutation as the negative of name —

$\qquad\qquad$ night's mutation is then cats (herd) — at night but not
changed by it

$\qquad\qquad$ one goes backward in night and utterly free — as in many or
any nights
(outside)
that is still one, I guess, but it doesn't seem to be — one doesn't
worry

$\qquad\qquad$ whenever I sit still and heard, it was worry — but going
backward it is night

$\qquad$ only. not from anything

$\qquad\qquad\qquad\qquad\qquad\qquad\qquad\qquad\qquad$ *(LS)*

$\qquad$ I can conceive of a subject for whom the sense of living
would be synonymous solely with a consciousness of 'passed and
missed experience.' Reality then would consist entirely of otherness
without transitions (the otherness consistent, unbreached). The
subject would never emerge — it would only survive, 'nothing now,'
blindness.

$\qquad$ But what makes me consider this eventless unfigured out
themeless subject unsusceptible to being undone or unnamed? Its
pure eventlessness springs out of silence but not out of night with
its cinematographic qualities — its guesswork and dreams. For the
real subject, time is construed out of guesswork and dreams
because out of them occupants do emerge. In fact, this 'real' subject
is an occupant (from 'something').

$\qquad\qquad\qquad\qquad\qquad\qquad\qquad\qquad\qquad$ *(LH)*

$\qquad\qquad\qquad\qquad\qquad$ ———

having to explode, detonate, power — because that is
oneself — real authority outside, of others

it is that not imposed

outside — one — one entirely different from the conflict
occurring

conflict not occurring in silence or night — being
redelineated to occur in one
transitions are it's being missed, to have occurred but not
now
nothing now is blindness occupants emerging — not rem,
event in spring

(LS)

Overwhelmed by the beauty of logical systems and
then even more by the beauty of reason — still one can't describe
this search as a guide to reality —
Or can one? reason bearing within it proximity to
experience, a threat of power, a narrative, and the curtain — some
sort of mental conflict occurring on any given evening as flutter on
the REM horizon — marvelously fluent
But easily bored?

Extravagant transmissions, fueled by things seen within a
day or two
Reflecting 'fishwife'
                            her lap full of 'aphrodisiac fish,' one
on another
                    becomes a memory

(LH)

I don't have any reason being circuit 'as dawn is' — jumping
— that is 'conflict' as itself horizon
or REM seen as reason/logic — which it is

extravagant transmissions, if they are outside,
           yet if they are 'conflict' in one seen to be 'incorrect'
so — jumps — as attempting then to correct as bring on to a
separate (?) circuit than dawn — ? — or to be one — seeing first,
before, is 'aphrodisiac fish' — one's 'through hoops' there being to
have *n o* conflict or to be 'in' conflict [only — one on another]
           rather — one in two, as 'aphrodisiac fish' [at the same time
           — one fish held on the bottom under emerges as two
[conflict as *n o* — none

                                                                (LS)

           Coming under the full moon from the building behind the
car a white dog showing, walking on its hind legs, simian (feigning
— something human) — (in real life REM logic reason warrants
['necessitates'] comedies [because they resolve] in conflict): dog in
a cloud, dog in a wallet, dog in tears, dog darting at flipping
aphrodisiac fish on slippery tiles among silver scales
           This is all valuable

           Good is meant by it: the sensation of the transition to other
experience, a metamorphosis of thought
           The hoop is a spectacle, (just) a mode

                                                                (LH)

           in *despair* — dogs flipping aphrodisiac fish — finally — as in
'fine' — isn't that 'one'
           'good' ('from'?) is meant by the sensation of transition — if
one is a dog in tears (one is
           formation is only one — and older ones go [die] — so a hoop
is racing red trees before
           flipping [as fish] — rem logic warrants one — 'there'

           'good' as 'logic' is from you so that is metamorphosis as
one's-real-outer-time-span-or-period-a-hoop

                                                                (LS)

As if wheeling on one's outer time span — it might be into battle and back again (this seems like a workable description of an epic) or some boisterous adventure as an entrepreneur during which one sees the landscape entirely transformed

It wouldn't matter whether the hero were good or bad; only action turns on the outer time span

Setting out

Orange beetles fly up — the human body also can produce color, as well as a series of frightening faces with which to punish a naughty child

Give a child seven words with which to invent a story 'on the spot'

From that spot the orange beetles fly up

It would be reprehensible to make less of the inner time span than takes place in a nightmare of secret buzzing

Is that (making sense) the erotic business of philosophy?

(LH)

My sister and I have a memory
of gigantic moths in a hot night on deck of a freighter
hitting the lights under which hundreds of stevedores work
on gangplank from huge black night — sleeping at night now
at present (yet we are separated,
the orange beetles fly up in blue — we are with people
I think the orange beetles fly only in future — 'will' as being
present —
— orange beetles are not within our knowledge — by nature
(so he says that is an inaccurate goal) — happy —

action which has occurred isn't philosophy — and is erotic —
so must be philosophy — also, — of children

Oppen said the women he knew didn't think space should
be investigated (investigating space the outside-the-human being
what's 'human') and therefore were / are subhuman — Quartermain
says 'it cannot be known', (shouldn't be — isn't — terrain — ?) "so
'women' are right"

one is 'women' wanting investigating space — 'it can
be known' (being [double] transgressing social

(LS)

'Perception of a vivid constellation' (criticism) 'requires correct distancing.'

Girls from the moon, in the 'new' position; comparisons begin here.

Are we close?

The perception of a work is bound to its position.

Waking, blinking, reflecting — securing double being: happiness (which can lead to a sense of unhappiness, even to illness (replacement)).

The metaphysical material can no longer be discerned through contemplation — girls from our times act accordingly

(LH)

After the flood — arctic swans floated and flew landing on the inland ocean where highway and green land are underneath.

At the same time — one's consciousness is cocooned. Later seems to burst from this and is very alert while (and as) seemingly only part of one. 'People can't take that direct observation' as if there *'weren't'* experience and it *'is' 'not'*

Observation or sight or critical being distinct from each other, faculties, and the swans being one's faculty — them. Not being one's own eyes or any eyes — and by this separation / this absence — (the swans floating on flood) one's direct faculty (as 'by' not being one).

Dismantling or sight or critical being distinct from each other, faculties, and the swans being one's faculty — them. Not being one's own eyes or any eyes — and by this separation — (the swans floating on flood) one's direct faculty (as 'by'/beside not being one).

Dismantling or dropping one's own primary early basis and seeing that is not occurring, cannot — as being what would be that occurring — is a state that is actually experienced 'outside' either material or contemplation.

(LS)

Taking the swan form in the 'flood' position, ring or rings
Taking oneself to the 'outside' of material contemplation,
where one is vulnerable to 'some enchantment'
Passing lakes, survivors — one (actually a vulture, who is
bathing in the river) tries but fails to capture swans
The swans *never* are dismantled, turning into girls, divested
of their feathers, in the form of women

Moving mimetically, 'fish-form'
Former women
Dragging steps to simulate being tailed
The surviving partners passing and repassing, taking turns at
being forward, to mimic the paths of fish in the water, blowing flood
Swallowed it — but not immediately — washing about
On stilts, flood
From introduction to denomination, description, and
distraction to conclusion

(LH)

They *are* dismantled —

then

(LS)

AERIAL/EDGE

They Beat Me Over the Head With a Sack, Anselm Berrigan, $5.

Integrity & Dramatic Life, Anselm Berrigan, $10.

the julia set, Jean Donnelly, $4.

Marijuana Softdrink, Buck Downs, forthcoming 1999.

World Prefix, Harrison Fisher, $4.

Metropolis 16-20, Rob Fitterman, $5.

perhaps this is a rescue fantasy, Heather Fuller, $10.

Sight, Lyn Hejinian and Leslie Scalapino, $12.

Late July, Gretchen Johnsen, $3.

Asbestos, Wayne Kline, $6.

Stepping Razor, A.L. Nielsen, $9.

Errata 5uite, Joan Retallack, $8.

Dogs, Phyllis Rosenzweig, $5.

Aerial 9: Bruce Andrews, Rod Smith ed., forthcoming 1998.

Aerial 8: Barrett Watten, Rod Smith ed., $15.

Aerial 6/7 featuring John Cage, Rod Smith ed., $15.

Aerial 5 featuring Harryman/Hejinian, Darragh/Retallack, Rod Smith ed., $7.50.

On Your Knees, Citizen: A Collection of "Prayers" for the "Public" [Schools], Rod Smith, Lee Ann Brown, and Mark Wallace, eds., $6.

Cusps, Chris Stroffolino, $2.50.

Nothing Happened and Besides I Wasn't There, Mark Wallace, $9.50.

Orders to: Aerial/Edge, POBox 25642, Washington, DC 20007.

Add $1 postage for individual titles. 2 or more books postpaid.